the soccer method

ATTACKING
DOWN THE FLANK

Henk Mariman

**Library of Congress
Cataloging - in - Publication Data**

the Soccer Method
Book 2 - Attacking Down the Flank
by Henk Mariman

ISBN-13: 978-1-59164-104-9
ISBN-10: 1-59164-104-7
Library of Congress Control Number: 2006903027
© 2006

Editing
Bryan R. Beaver

Translation from Dutch
Dave Brandt

Printed by
Data Reproductions
Auburn, Michigan

Reedswain Publishing
562 Ridge Road
Spring City, PA 19475
www. reedswain.com
info@reedswain.com

Contents

Introduction

Wing play has changed considerably in modern adult soccer. Genuinely creative wingers have become a rarity. Technically gifted wingers have made way for other types of players. Wide players are often midfielders rather than attackers, and the play on the flanks involves more running and/or combination plays. The sight of a winger taking on a full back is less common.

The effectiveness of wingers has been debated in recent years. Due to the scarcity of "genuine" wingers, many coaches have abandoned the traditional formation with 3 attackers. The use of attacking wingers has also been questioned. As a result of these developments, fewer runs with the ball are made down the flank.

Sadly this development has also manifested itself in youth soccer. Here, too, one against one duels on the flank are disappearing, and this is unfortunate.

The development of young soccer players requires a totally different approach from that of result-oriented adult soccer. Adult wing play differs greatly from wing play in youth soccer. The pressure to win puts wing play into a different context.

If the coach of an adult team has no creative players available, he must find other solutions. These are governed by the need to get quick results. In practice, the flank players are given a more defensively oriented role and the flank is left more open. Depending on the qualities of the players, other ways of exploiting the flanks are sought. Coaches of adult teams assess the qualities of the players and, depending on their strong and weak points, he assigns them specific roles. These are roles in which the players can best serve the interests of the team as a whole, because the performance of the team as a whole is what matters most in adult soccer.

In youth soccer, the first priority is the individual development of the players. A role is assigned to a player because it will further his development. The situations he faces in this role can have a favorable influence on his individual development. A winger who has problems dribbling past an opponent can be confronted with lots of 1v1 situations. Because the match result is less important, the coach has more time to invest in the individual players. The young age of the players also offers the coach more options for making progress.

The way in which the coach influences a player depends on the player's age. As the players grow older, the situations they are confronted with bear more resemblance to situations in adult soccer, but there must always be room for further individual development and for 1v1 situations.

Variations and run lines offer opportunities for development in youth soccer as well as adult soccer. However, creative individual development must never be put at risk.

THE CONTENTS OF THIS BOOK

After reading this book, a coach should be able to incorporate wing play into his training sessions. I have divided the wing play module into six sections.

Section 1: All typical aspects of wing play that need to be worked on ("work items") are collected here. I have distilled the most important work items from the numerous soccer matches I have watched between teams of young players.

In **section 2**, I define the tasks and functions of the total team, the lines of the team (defense, midfield, attack) and the specific positions (based on a 1-3-4-3 team formation).

In **section 3**, I describe all the aims of wing play. These aims are aligned to the chosen playing system.

Section 4 deals with the ball skills needed during wing play. These techniques are linked to coaching points and practice drills. Young soccer players can be coached in 2 ways. The players can learn about the aims of the game, and they can learn about the specific soccer problems revealed by analyzing real matches.

In **section 5**, I explain more about this.

Section 6 contains specific drills. The level of these drills is adapted to the different age groups.

Work Items

THE POSITION OF THE WINGER

The winger stands too far infield

Wingers move infield too often. This means that they are not available for passes to the flank, or the play cannot be switched from one flank to the other. In many cases the ball is played out to the wing anyway, and the winger then has to chase after it, facing the flank; he therefore cannot see what is happening on the field, and valuable time is also lost.

The winger stands too deep

By standing too deep, or coming toward the ball too soon, the winger closes down the available space. Not only does he have less time to control the ball but he has fewer options, in view of the number of opponents in the restricted space.

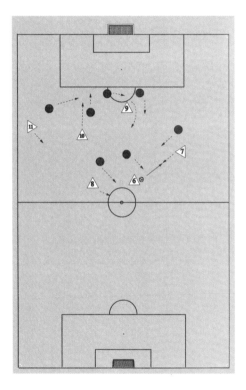
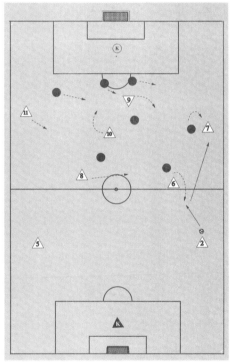

There is too little variation

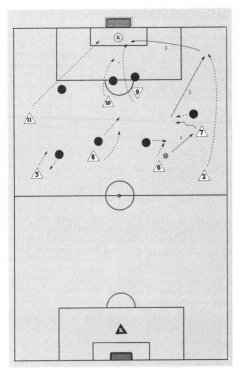

The winger fails to dribble past his opponent. Although too few chances are created by playing down the flank, the team does not change its manner of playing and is therefore too predictable. Neither the midfielder nor the winger takes the initiative.

The ball is not played forward often enough

The moments when the winger is in space and available are limited. The defenders and the midfielders play the ball around aimlessly, without any intention of playing it forward.

Although the winger is in space, he comes toward the ball

The winger is in space on the flank. His marker is at a safe distance. Instead of staying put, he comes toward the ball. This wastes time.

One winger has the ball and the other winger doesn't think ahead

The right winger starts a run with the ball. The left winger stays on the flank.

The opposing team plays very defensively. It is therefore more difficult to pass to the wingers than in other games. The wingers don't try hard enough to make themselves available.

PASSING AND CONTROLLING THE BALL

The ball is played to the flank too frequently

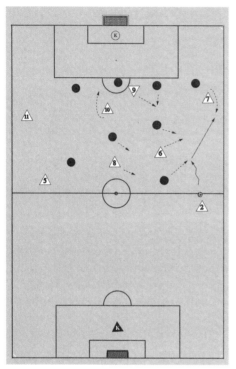

A pass from the infield to the flank can be easily dealt with by defenders. Due to the proximity of the sideline, there are few escape options.

The team plays too often and too long on the same flank

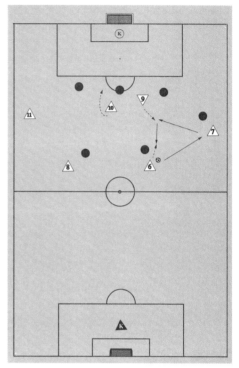

If the play is restricted to one flank for too long, the opposing team is able to organize and pressure the ball. Opportunities for creating goal-scoring chances are minimal.

There is no cooperation between the winger and the midfielder

The midfielder passes to the winger, but there is no cooperation between the two. The midfielder fails to support the winger.

The ball reaches the winger too slowly

The winger is in space but his teammates take too long to play the ball to him. The ball is circulated too long, the players' speed of execution is too slow, too many players are involved in passing sequences.

The winger's first touch is poor

The winger's first touch is poor, giving the defender the opportunity to get into the right position or win the ball.

The winger is positioned wrongly to receive the ball

The winger receives the ball, but is standing with his back to the opposing team's goal (instead of to the sideline). He therefore cannot see what is happening on the field behind him. After controlling the ball, he needs more time to size up his next move.

The point of attack is not varied

The right winger makes a run with the ball. The opposing defenders are well organized and close down the space ahead of him. The winger keeps trying to force an opening and the players behind him (right midfielder and right back) are not brought into play to switch the point of attack.

The wingers keep the ball too long

The winger has the ball. Although there is no way forward, he keeps possession. This gives the opposing team time to organize and pressure the ball.

THE 1v1 SITUATION

The winger cannot dribble past the defender

The ball is played to the winger, who cannot dribble past the defender.

The winger makes no attempt to dribble past the defender

Although he is faced by only one defender, the winger makes no attempt to dribble past him.

The winger takes the ball past the defender, but allows him to challenge again

The defender always manages to recover and challenge the winger again after the winger takes the ball past him.

The winger does not dribble past the defender on the outside

The winger fakes to go past the defender on the outside, but ultimately always tries to pass him on the inside.

The continuation after the winger has taken the ball past the defender is ineffective

The winger goes past the defender but the continuation, whether it is a pass to a teammate or a cross, is poor.

The winger is not interested in running onto passes played down the flank ahead of him

The winger always expects the ball played to his feet. He does not want the ball to be played into space ahead of him.

THE CROSS AND THE POSITIONS IN FRONT OF THE GOAL

The winger crosses too early
The winger only watches the ball and crosses without first sizing up the situation in front of the goal.

The winger crosses too late
There is a lot of space between the defenders and the goal. The winger could easily play the ball into this space, but instead he takes the ball further forward and crosses as he approaches the end line.

There is no one at the near post
The cross is hit hard to the near post. The attacker in front of the goal arrives too late or fails to get in front of the defender or the goalkeeper.

The winger uses the wrong technique when he crosses
The winger crosses with the inside of the foot (the instep). The technique is not suited to the situation.

There are too few options in front of the goal
The winger has too few options. There are no attackers in the penalty area or they are not available.

The cross is too easily intercepted

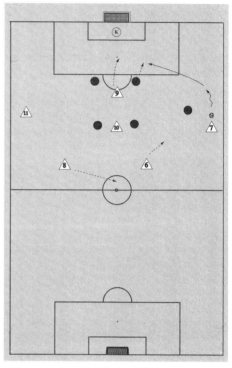

- The cross is too high or too low
- The ball is not struck firmly enough
- The path of the ball is too straight or too easy to intercept

There is too little determination in front of the goal
The attackers in front of goal lack the "over my dead body" mentality. They are too careless with their chances and react too slowly to be first to the rebound.

Tasks and functions

THE CROSS AND THE POSITIONS IN FRONT OF THE GOAL

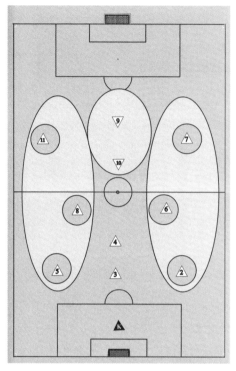

elements cannot be described in terms of tasks and functions. The tasks and functions described here are more a framework for the coach than a target to be achieved.

More specific tips for each age category are given in section 5. The emphasis is on the roles of the players who are chiefly involved in wing play.

I have chosen a 1-3-4-3 system, to which I have linked a way of playing. Within each system and the associated way of playing, there are tasks and functions for the team as a whole, the lines (defense, midfield, attack) and the individual positions. The tasks and functions in this description are totally oriented to the development of young soccer players.

Age plays a key role here. The tasks and functions differ for each age group. The tasks and functions described here are aimed at 15 to 18-year-olds. Coaches of other age groups can integrate those tasks and functions that are suitable for their own players.

By describing the tasks and functions, I am not putting the players in a straightjacket. Wing play should not be stereotyped. Chances are created via the flank by making runs, taking initiatives and interchanging positions. These

TASKS FOR THE WHOLE TEAM (ATTACKING)

- Make the playing area as large as possible (length and width).
- Don't stand too close together or too far apart.
- Try to create dangerous situations in the opposing team's penalty area as quickly as possible, without neglecting the philosophy of retaining the ball.
- Create opportunities to play passes forward (to run on to) or to feet.
- Take up good positions in front of the goal when the ball is crossed.

TASKS FOR THE INDIVIDUAL LINES (ATTACKING)

Defensive line
- No unnecessary loss of possession in your own half.
- Circulate the ball quickly.
- Try to switch the play as quickly as possible.
- Try to play the ball forward as quickly as possible.
- Try to play the ball to teammates in space.
- Take up good positions relative to your teammates.
- Use the space well relative to the opposing team's strikers.
- Communicate.

Midfield line
- Read the game.
- Take up positions that allow the ball to be played forward into attacking zones, or take up positions where you can receive the ball.
- Support your strikers.
- Fast play (one-touch play – good ball control – take up good positions).
- Don't run forward too early.
- Take over each other's positions.
- Create dangerous situations as quickly as possible by:
  - Shooting at the goal
  - Playing the ball into the space between the defenders and the goalkeeper
  - Playing the ball forward to the striker/wingers
  - Playing the ball forward to the withdrawn striker

- Switching the play from one flank to the other
- Taking up a position on the edge of the penalty area for a cross

Attacking line
- Good cooperation between the striker and the withdrawn striker.
- Take up positions that allow the ball to be played forward into attacking zones.
- Good movement (run toward the ball, then check away again).
- Keep the playing area as large as possible (wingers stay on the flank).
- Vary your runs into space so they are not predictable. Create space for individual runs with the ball.
- Be aware of the third man.
- Don't move toward the ball too early.
- Take up good positions in front of the goal for a cross.
- Remember that the aim is to create chances and score goals.

9

TASKS PER POSITION (ATTACKING)

Right and left backs (2 and 5)
- Fan out toward the flanks.
- Be ready to react quickly if possession is lost.
- Be aware of what is happening in the attacking zone and play the ball to your attackers if you can.
- Look out for opportunities to pass the ball forward into attacking zones.
- Support the winger.
- Keep possession if build-up down the flank is not possible.
- Communicate with the players on the flank (6/8/7/11).
- Try to overlap the winger if the game situation allows it.

Midfielders (6 and 8)
- Try to create opportunities to pass the ball forward into attacking zones.
- Support the strikers.
- Do not make a forward run too soon.
- Keep the play under control.
- Focus on creating chances.
- Good positional play relative to the other players.
- Take up a position on the edge of the penalty area for a cross
- Don't close down the space in front of you by moving forward into it.
- Switch the ball from the center of the field to the winger.
- Try to overlap the winger if the game situation allows it.
- Create space for individual runs with the ball.

The withdrawn striker (10)
- Alternate supporting role and overlapping role.
- Be available to receive a lay-off from the striker.
- Don't take up positions too far forward.
- Good positional play relative to the other players.
- Be available.
- Use the space created by the striker.
- Get into scoring positions.
- Remember that the aim is to score goals.
- Be aware of the third man.

- Take up good positions in front of the goal for a cross.

The striker (9)
- Remember that the aim is to score goals.
- Read the build-up play.
- Try to get into scoring positions.
- Be available.
- Play forcefully in the attacking zone.
- Don't just lay the ball off; make runs with the ball too.
- Make space for the other players.
- Be aware of the third man.
- Take up good positions in front of the goal.

The wingers (7 and 11)
- Be available to receive the ball on the flank.
- Make runs with the ball or join in combination plays with the aim of crossing the ball.
- Time your runs with the ball well.
- Take up good positions in front of the goal when the ball is crossed from the other flank.
- Be aware of the situation in front of the goal before you cross the ball.
- Remember that the aim is to create chances and score goals.

The aims of the game

ATTACKING DOWN THE FLANK

The game of soccer can be broken down into 3 situations: own team in possession, opposing team in possession, and change of possession. Possession can in turn be broken down into 2 phases:

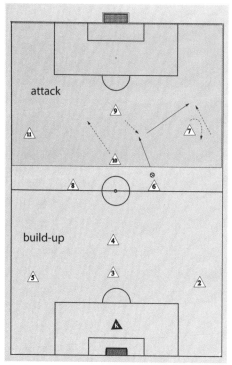

The build-up is the preparation for the attack. The players try to get the ball forward purposefully and efficiently. Build-up play from the back takes place in the team's own half and around the center circle.

The aims of the game must be translated into practice to promote the individual development of the players rather than just to get a result.

The wing play module deals specifically with attacking play down the flanks by, in particular, the wingers, midfielders and full backs in cooperation with the striker and withdrawn striker.

To achieve this, we must look at attacking play down the flank in detail. In this section we explain the basics of wing play in a manner that furthers the players' development.

I discuss the most common aims of wing play and principles of attacking down the flank.

The aims of wing play

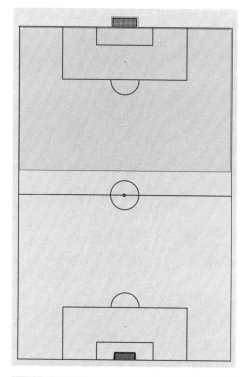

Aims:
- To create dangerous situations in the opposing team's penalty area.
- To score goals.

By:
- Individual runs with the ball, combination play, forward passes and shots at goal.
- Crossing the ball.

The decisive phases of wing play

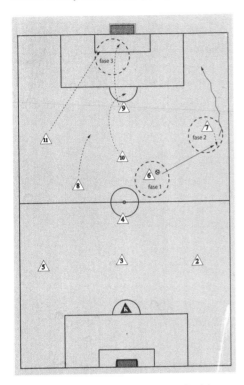

Phase 1: Creating a chance on the flank by means of an individual run with the ball, a combination or a variation.
Phase 2: Crossing the ball.
Phase 3: Positions in front of the goal.

The execution of these 3 phases determines the efficiency of the wing play.

Flank variations

Flank play can vary in several ways. The varia-tions offer the players a number of options, without imposing rigidly drilled run lines. Chances can be created from the flank in 6 different ways.

Variation 1: Pass to winger; winger makes a run with the ball

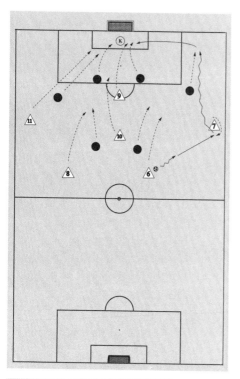

Runs with the ball are a fundamental part of wing play

- The winger checks away and back again to create space.
- The ball is passed to the winger, who uses the outside foot to control it.
- The winger makes a run with the ball.

Variation 2: Pass to winger; winger plays ball back to passer, who plays it forward for him to run onto

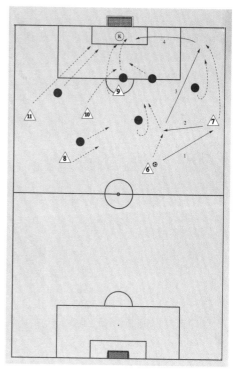

- The winger checks away and back again to create space.
- The ball is played to his right foot and he passes it back with his first touch.
- He then sprints forward and the ball is played into his path.

Don't vary the play just for the sake of it. It is better to play a few variations well rather than trying out pointless combinations.

Variation 3: Forward ball down the flank

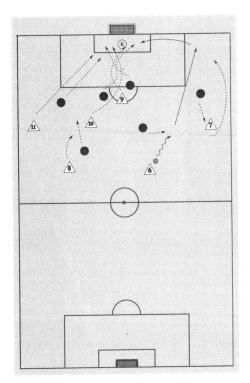

Variation 4: Ball to feet; create space; return pass to feet

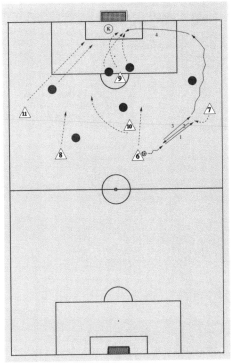

- The winger darts toward the ball; his marker follows.
- This creates space behind the marker.
- The ball is played into the space for the winger to run onto.

The forward pass into space tends not to be used often during training sessions. Coaches generally prefer the ball to be played to feet. Nevertheless, since the first priority is to get the ball forward into the attacking zone, this variation must be practiced during training sessions.

The forward pass into the attacking zone is the first priority.

- The winger darts away from the ball, which is then played to his right foot.
- He is closely marked and plays the ball back to the passer.
- He creates space by sprinting forward, and calls for the ball.
- The ball is played to his feet, then he turns and makes a run with the ball.

"If a winger receives the ball in a good position and tries to dribble past his marker, it is not so terrible if he loses the ball. In principle he has a 50-50 chance; either he takes the ball past his marker or he loses it. If he is in form, he will usually go past his marker. If he is not, he can always restrict himself to his basic task."

John Van't Schip, Ajax Amsterdam

15

Variation 5: The winger moves infield and creates space for another player

Variation 6: The winger cuts infield and the ball is played into his path

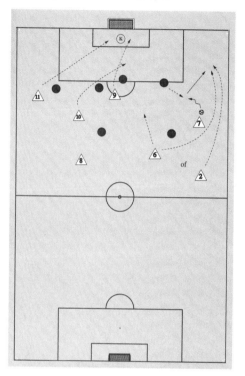

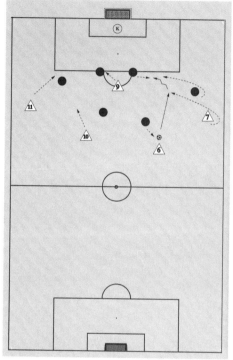

- The winger moves infield, either with or without the ball, and creates space for the player making a forward run down the flank.

Options:
- A defender (2/5) makes the forward run.
- A midfielder (6/8) makes a diagonal run behind the winger and advances down the flank.

- Cutting inside from the flank is one of the most difficult runs to master.
- The winger draws the defender towards the sideline and then cuts inside at exactly the right moment.
- He cuts across the path of the defender.

These variations can be demonstrated in a passing and shooting drill during the first phase of the training session. They can then be practiced with real opponents, as it is the opponents who determine where the available space is.

"The flank used to be the territory of a gifted technical player with a lot of insight, but now the full back is a semi-midfielder who is a strong runner. My view is that this is the right place for a player who can cope well in tight situations, because he can use his technique for 95% of what he does."

Johan Cruyff

"When I have dribbled past 4 of them, it is only 7 against 11!"

Faas Wilkes

The winger chooses position

Creating space

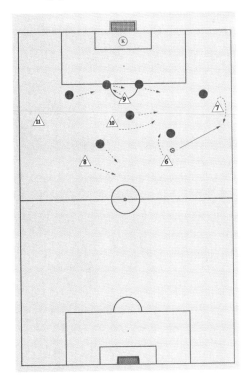

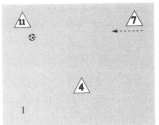

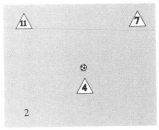

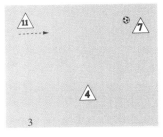

One of the main tasks of a winger is to create space. Staying on the flank makes more space available. Wingers often stand too far infield, and are therefore less accessible. The position of a winger depends on his skills.

Some examples:

- A player who prefers to beat his opponent on the inside will move inside more often. This leaves space on the flank.
- A left-footer on the right or a right-footer on the left will naturally tend to move inside. Other players can then make use of the space left on the flank.
- A genuine winger will prefer to beat his man on the outside. He can exploit 1v1 situations more effectively.

It is important for young players to try out all the aspects they can. They should not be prematurely stuck with a specific position. It is better to respect a player's individuality and encourage him to play the role that comes most naturally.

In principle, both players should take up position closer to the sideline when the ball is in the center (Diagram 2). When the left winger has the ball, the right winger should move further infield (Diagram 1). If the ball is switched from one flank to the other, he has sufficient time to move back toward the sideline, but if the left winger makes a run with the ball and plays a cross, the right winger has less distance to cover before he arrives in front of goal. A winger who keeps moving has more chance of escaping the attention of a defender than one who remains static on the flank.

17

The position of the winger when play is built up from the back

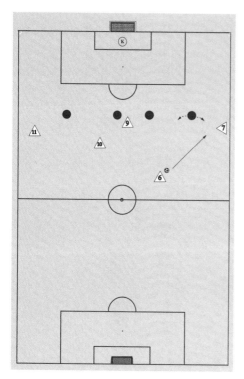

The winger takes up a position as far forward as possible. This has the following advantages:

- His direct opponent cannot mark him closely, as there would then be too large a gap between the full back and the central defender.
- The central defender cannot cover the full back to the same extent as he can when the winger hangs back.
- By taking up a forward position, the winger leaves more space free in the central third of the pitch. The full backs (2 and 5) can therefore pass more easily to players in the center.

The winger should stand with his back to the sideline

Photo 1
Winger with back to sideline

Photo 2
Winger with back to opponent

The winger stands with his back to the sideline so that he can more easily turn with the ball or play it back with his first touch and he can see the entire field (Photo 1). If the winger stands with his back to his opponent it is more difficult to play the ball infield and he has fewer options.

Taking up position on the sideline

When the winger takes up position on the sideline, he reduces his options (no space in which to dribble past his opponent on the outside. He should stand a few yards away from the sideline. He can then dribble past his opponent on either side.

Asking for the ball

The winger checks away

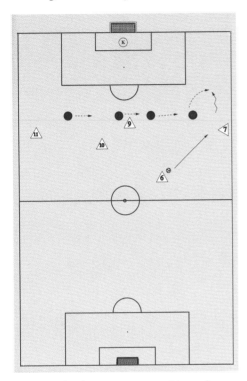

A winger checks away to escape his marker or create space. In the diagram the winger (7) is standing well forward. When he receives the ball from the midfielder, he can turn and run down the flank with it. If the sequence is performed quickly (pass, control, turn and run), the winger can cut across the defender's run line. If, however, the winger chooses to check away from the defender in this situation, and thus move a few yards toward the ball, the defender has the chance to get into a covering position. A player who is in space has no need to check away toward the ball.

Checking away toward the ball

Checking away from the ball

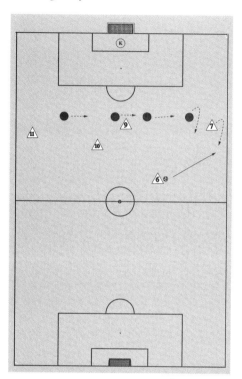
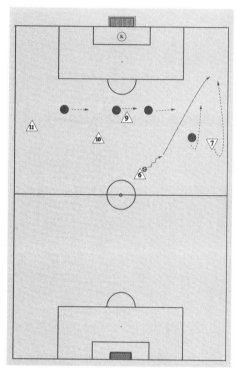

The winger draws the defender toward the ball, thus creating a few yards of space behind the defender.

The winger draws the defender away from the ball, thus giving himself a few yards' start on the defender.

Tips:
- The winger should stand with his weight on the front of his feet.
- This enables him to react faster.
- Start the check away with the foot closest to the sideline.
- Maintain eye contact with player in possession.
- The check away must be unexpected.
- The check away often only needs to be one step or a few yards.

Receiving the ball

With the outside foot

With the inside foot

The advantage here is that the player has his back to the sideline and can see the entire field. Receiving the ball with the outside foot is especially advantageous when the winger is facing his opponent.

This is advantageous when the winger can control the ball and run forward with it. The pass covers a shorter distance and can therefore be controlled a fraction of a second faster. The disadvantage is that there is a slightly greater risk that the ball will go out of play.

Tips:

- The outside foot should preferably be used to receive the ball.
- If this is too risky, use the inside foot.
- The winger should preferably be in motion when he receives the ball.
- If possible, the winger should control the ball in such a way that it can be played forward (depends on the defender).
- If no defender is nearby, the winger can control the ball and push it forward in one movement.

"It does not matter which foot is used to receive the ball. If it is played in the right direction, that is good enough for me."

Danny Blind

Passing to the winger

The effectiveness of the player in possession can be looked at in terms of the following assessments:

1. He creates opportunities for releasing the winger.
2. He keeps attacking moves flowing and seeks openings for creating chances.
3. He holds onto the ball and creates very few chances.
4. He rarely gets forward.
5. He loses possession too often.

Passes should communicate information. The speed and path of the ball can tell the winger what to do next.

The ball should preferably be played to the winger as far forward as possible. In practice this means that a forward pass for the winger to run onto is the first choice. During training sessions, however, the focus is often on passing to the winger's feet. As a result, passing into space is often neglected to some extent during real games.

Practical examples:

Passing toward the winger

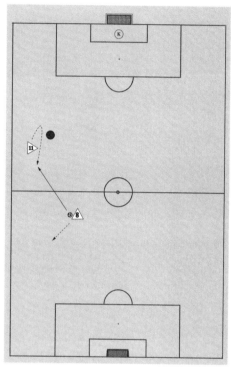

The defender is marking the winger (11) very closely. The ball can neither be played to the winger's feet nor down the flank for him to run onto. The left midfielder (8) plays the ball toward the winger. The defender cannot get to the ball first and the winger has time to control the ball. The midfielder must not pass the ball too firmly.

Too little attention is paid to passing down the flank.

Playing the ball into the path of the winger

Playing the ball into space

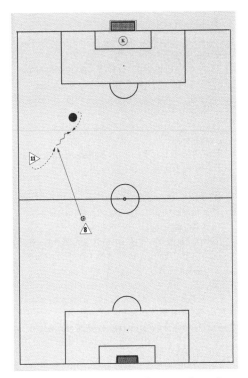

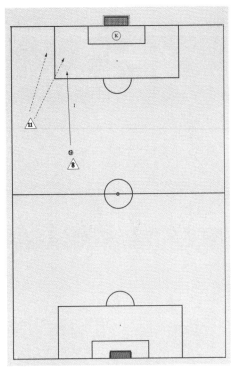

The defender is sufficiently far away from the winger. The left midfielder can play the ball into the path of the winger (11), who therefore receives the ball when he is in motion.

A long ball is often played into space near the corner of the field. The winger therefore has to play a difficult long cross. Long forward passes should be aimed as close to the goal as possible. In this situation the midfielder can best play the ball straight down the field (line 1). The distance to the goal is then shorter and the ball is more difficult for the defenders to intercept.

Tips:

a) Before playing the ball to the winger
- There should be eye contact between the player in possession and the winger.
- Make sure the ball is not played too close to the defender.

b) When the ball is played to the winger
- Play the ball firmly, so it is easier to control.
- Call to the winger before passing.
- Try to use the right technique. Each situation has to be approached on its own merits.

c) After passing to the winger
- Support the winger.

Coaching keywords	
Play	*Play the ball*
You're free	*No opponent nearby*
Lay it off	*Return the ball first touch*
Play it back	*Pass the ball back*
Forward	*Pass the ball upfield*
Deep	*Play the ball long*

The midfielders' tasks

The complexity of the midfield

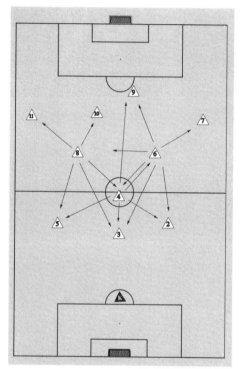

The midfield positions are the most difficult on the field. In view of their central positions, midfielders have to develop a lot of insight. A midfielder must learn positional play relative to the players in front of him (attackers), players outside of him (wingers) and players behind him (defenders). They have to be aware of everything happening in the 360 degrees around them! This makes life difficult. In view of the positional requirements on midfielders, coaching in build-up play is essential. The coach must stimulate the midfielders and give them a framework that encourages them without submerging their own individuality.

Individual requirements on midfielders

1. The main objective is to create dangerous situations in front of the opposing team's goal.
2. They must be able to take up good positions relative to the opposing players and the ball. Through their positional play, they create more options when in possession.
3. They must make one-touch passes as often as possible.
4. They must have a good ball control to allow them to create more passing options.
5. They must be able to communicate through their passes.
6. Midfielders must be able to think one or two steps ahead.
7. Midfielders must be able to maintain good positional balance relative to each other.
8. Midfielders must be able to maintain a good balance between the numbers of players in front of and behind the ball.

Collective requirements on midfielders

Facilitate flank play by:

- Creating space to enable the ball to be passed wide and forward.
- Supporting defenders, attackers and each other.
- Switching the play to the other flank.
- Making runs off the ball.
- Making runs with the ball.

a) Supporting the winger

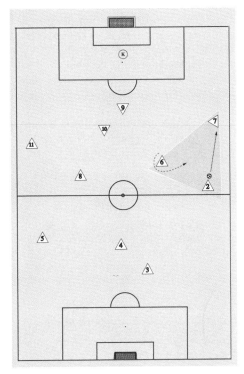

When the midfielder goes to support the winger, he must keep his distance. If he gets too close, his direct marker may follow and the players will have less space and time.

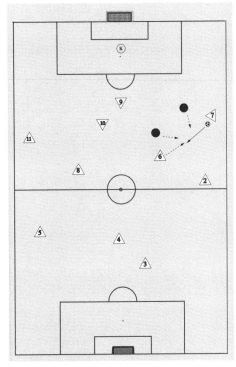

The right midfielder (6) comes toward the ball as the right back (2) passes to the right winger (7). When the winger receives the ball, the right midfielder is available to support him (the 3 players form a triangle).

The ball can only be played infield from the flank if the opposing players leave sufficient space.

When the midfielder receives the ball, he must give himself as many options as possible. If he receives the ball under his body or too far toward the flank, this may reduce his options (e.g. unable to switch the ball to the other flank). The manner in which he receives the ball is naturally also influenced by the opposing players.

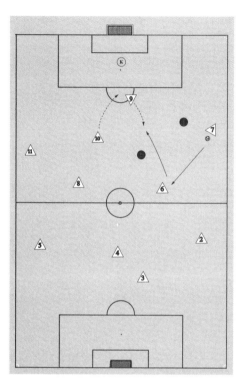

Too much time is often lost when the winger passes the ball to the midfielder. The midfielder can save time by looking ahead. If he sees an opportunity to play in the striker or the withdrawn striker, he can play the ball forward immediately. The pass to the striker is less easy for the defenders to predict and the striker has more time to control the ball.

b) Switching to the other flank

In some situations the opposing team exerts a lot of pressure on the flank where the ball is. As a result, there is often no possibility of creating chances on this flank. By switching the ball to the other flank, the team in possession creates more space for itself and there are more opportunities to create chances.

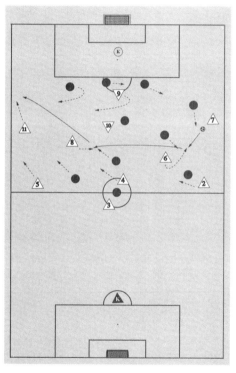

The manner of switching the flank depends on the level of skill of the midfielder and the resulting options. A midfielder with a good positional sense and good passing skills will be able to create one or more options. The positions of his teammates and the opposing players also play a role. A number of possible scenarios for switching to the other flank follow.

Options
Priority goes to getting the ball as far forward as possible

In the opposition's half, the best option is always to create a chance. If the midfielder receives a pass back from the winger, creating a dangerous situation in or around the penalty area is always the first choice. If this is not possible, the ball should be switched to the other flank as quickly as possible. Priority is always given to getting the ball as far forward as possible on the other flank. If the most advanced player on the other flank is not available, other players can act as intermediate links, depending on the positions of teammates and opponents.

- First choice = Pass to the most advanced player (e.g. the winger).
- Second choice = Pass to another player as an intermediate link.

Try to reach the winger as far forward as possible using one of the following options, in the given order of priority:
1. Forward pass into space.
2. Pass to feet.
3. Away from the defender, behind the winger.

The best option must be chosen as quickly as possible.

Switching to the other flank directly

We try to play the ball to the winger as quickly as possible. The faster the player on the wing receives the ball, the more time and space are gained.

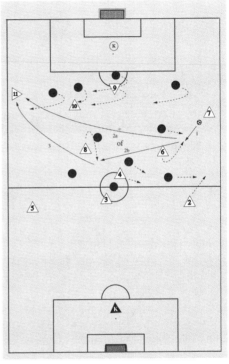

The right midfielder (6) receives the ball from the right winger (7) and passes directly to the left winger (11). If the left winger is not available, the left midfielder (8) can act as an intermediate link.

This ball is useful if the defender presses toward the flank and sufficient space is created for playing the ball. The manner in which the midfielder receives the ball depends on his level of skill (can he use both feet?), his position when he receives the ball and the positions of the opposing players.

Running back toward your own goal and then calling for the ball is the most difficult way of creating space.

If his marker leaves sufficient space, he can receive the ball with his left foot and pass with his right foot (Photo 1).

If his marker is closer, he can turn and pass with his left foot (Photo 2).

Direct passing to the other flank occurs more frequently from age 13. Younger players need more intermediate links.

Switching to the other flank via an intermediate link

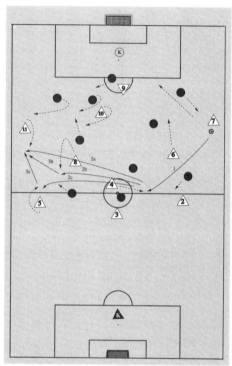

The right midfielder (6) creates space for the central midfielder (4) by making a forward run without the ball. The central midfielder receives the ball from the right winger (7) and passes immediately to the left winger (11). The left midfielder (8) makes a forward run to leave a free path for the pass to the winger.

If the central midfielder (4) cannot pass to the winger, he can use the left midfielder (8) or the left back (5) as an intermediate link.

Switching to the other flank via the attackers *c) Creating space for the wingers*

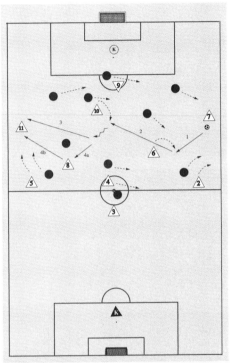 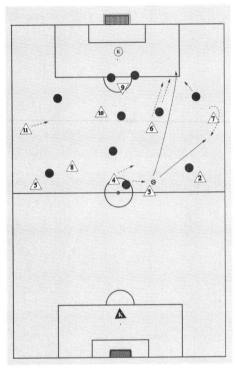

The right midfielder (6) receives the ball from the right winger (7) and passes to the striker (9) or withdrawn striker (10), who, if his marker allows him sufficient space, tries to reach the left winger (11). If this is too risky, he can pass to the left midfielder (8). A square pass to a winger is only an option if there is no risk of an interception.

The right midfielder (6) makes a run without the ball between the striker (9) and the winger (7). The right winger's marker will tend to move infield to cover, leaving more space for the right winger. The right midfielder (6) draws his marker with him toward the ball before making his forward run.

*Creating space for the winger from a central
position, then moving up in support*

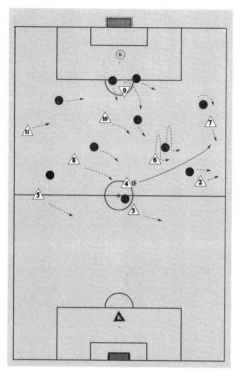

The right midfielder (6) makes a forward run
without the ball, drawing his marker with
him. This creates space for a pass to the right
winger (7) from a central position. When the
winger (7) has the ball, the right midfielder (6)
drops back to support him.

THE CROSS

A winger is not judged by the number of times he takes the ball past an opponent. His productivity depends mainly on his crosses. A winger does not always have to dribble past an opponent before he makes a good cross.

Crossing is a skill in itself. Few wingers have this skill naturally. We can encourage crossing as part of the soccer education of young players. The ability to use this skill is, however, age related. Not every age group has the strength or coordination to play a long cross.

The youngest players can cross from a shorter distance. The winger moves inside and has 3 options:

- Cross to the near post
- Cross to the far post
- Pull the ball back towards the edge of the penalty area.

From the age of about 13 the players are stronger and are capable of crossing from a longer distance. It is important that sufficient attention is given to crossing the ball at this age. A dangerous ball across the front of the goal is a formidable weapon.

Tips:

Before crossing
- Push the ball firmly forward if no opponent is nearby.
- Keep the ball close to your feet if an opponent is nearby.
- After dribbling past an opponent, cut across his path.
- Keep an eye on the players in front of the goal.
- Look at the goalkeeper's position. If he stands at the near post, for example, there are opportunities at the far post.
- It is not necessary to dribble past an opponent before crossing.
    - Sometimes all you need to do to create the space needed to cross the ball is drag it toward the flank
    - If your direct opponent leaves sufficient space, you can cross the ball from the sideline.

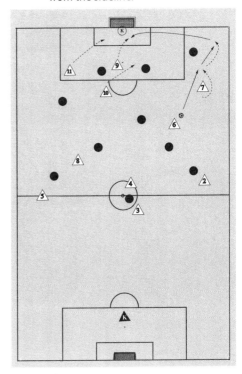

Technique
- It is easier to cross the ball if you push it forward diagonally a short distance infield first.
- Face diagonally toward the opposing goal.
- It is easier to cross the ball if you slow down slightly before striking it.
- Strike the ball with the inside of the instep; the harder the ball is crossed, the more difficult it is to intercept.
- A firm, inswinging cross is hardest to defend against.
- Keep an eye on the situation in front of the goal; remain calm.

Types of cross:
Cross from the end line

Crossing from the end line has some advantages:
- The attacker can run onto the ball.
- The defenders have to run toward their own goal and then turn to run away from the goal. This switch gives the attackers more space.

Disadvantage
- If the defenders have more time, they can organize to deal with the cross and it is more difficult to reach an attacker.

- *Cross to the near post*
  - Firm and low – waist-high or head-high.
  - Preferably the ball should not bounce.
  - Place the cross in front of the goalkeeper.
  - Keep the ball moving quickly.

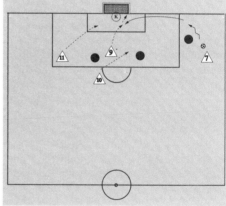

- The cut back from the end line
- Into the space in front of the attacker in front of the goal.
- To the correct foot.
- Sufficient pace on the ball.
- The ball should not bounce.

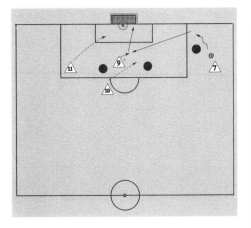

- Cross that drops to the far post
- Over the goalkeeper
- Firm
- Not too high, with sufficient pace on the ball.
- Attacker tries to score or lays the ball back.

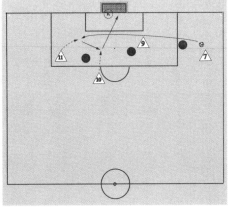

The players often lack sharpness when carrying out finishing drills. Try to encourage the players to adopt a competitive attitude during training sessions.

Cross into the space between the defenders and the goalkeeper

If there is sufficient space between the goalkeeper and the defenders, playing a quick cross into this space can be very effective. Because there are gaps between the defenders and the attackers, the player can quickly put the ball where he wants it. The defenders are still running back and are not organized. Wingers often tend to run to the end line without noticing that there is space behind the defenders.

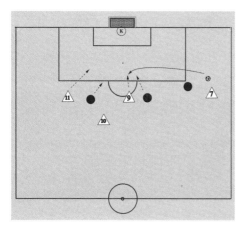

POSITION IN FRONT OF GOAL

Players of all ages can be coached on where to stand in front of goal. More attention should be focused on this from the age of 13.

Tips:

- Run diagonally into the line of the ball.

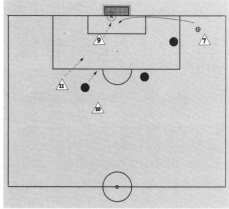

By running diagonally into the line of the ball, an attacker can head the ball more easily (the player's head is more or less behind the ball). If the attacker runs in along the same line as the ball, he has only a fraction of a second to head it.

- The players stand diagonally behind each other

- The winger has several options

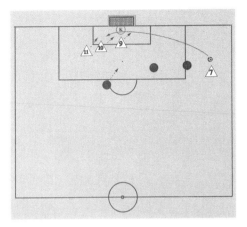

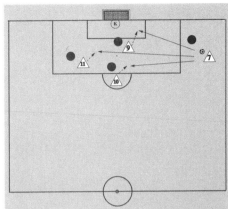

Some coaches ask their players to run in after each other in a diagonal line. When the cross comes over, the attacking team therefore has three chances in succession. The disadvantage is that an opposing player who is strong in the air may be positioned at the front of the line; the winger then has few other options for crossing the ball.

In this case the players stand more or less in a triangle. The winger can therefore cross the ball in one of 3 different directions.

- *Do not let the defender know where you are going to cross until the last possible moment*

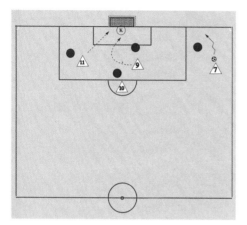

- *Get in front of the goalkeeper*

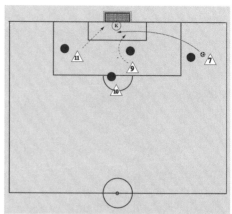

The striker (9) darts toward the far post to create space, then changes direction and runs into the space he has created. Depending on where he chooses to stand in front of goal, there are other options.

If the player at the near post runs in behind the goalkeeper, the goalkeeper can catch the ball more easily.

Don't forget the rebound!

- There should always be a player at the near post and at the far post
- It is easier to run forward than backward.
- Do not run in too soon.
- Run at an angle to the line of the ball.

Variations in front of goal:

Variation 1:

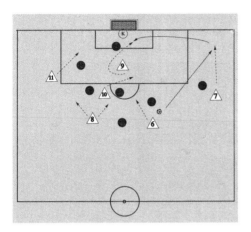

Variation 2:

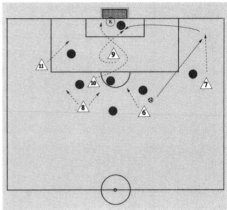

- The striker (9) checks away toward the far post, then darts toward the near post.
- The withdrawn striker (10) runs diagonally behind him, ready for a cross toward the penalty spot.
- The left winger (11) moves infield and takes up position at the far post.
- The midfielders (6 and 8) cover the penalty area, ready to pick up the ball if it is cleared.

- The striker (9) checks away toward the far post, then darts toward the near post.
- The withdrawn striker (10) checks away toward the near post, then darts toward the far post, crossing with the striker (9).
- The left winger (11) moves infield and takes up position at the far post.
- The midfielders (6 and 8) cover outside the penalty area, ready to pick up the ball if it is cleared. One of them can push forward to receive a lay back.

If the cross does not come, more variation can be tried. The left winger (11) can choose to run in toward the near post.

Variation 3:

- The players position themselves in front of goal.
- The left winger (11) runs across the goal to the near post.
- The withdrawn striker (10) takes up position at the far post.
- The striker (9) drops back to be able to receive a pull-back toward the penalty spot.

Variation 2:

- The moment for an attacker to lose his marker is when the marker looks toward the ball.

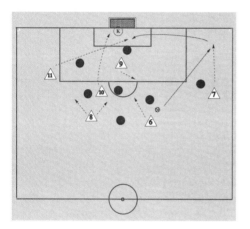

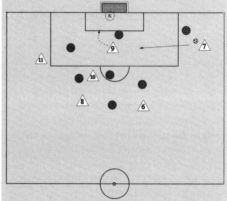

- When an attacker runs in at the near post, it is important to be just in front of the defender. The attacker can then cut across the defender's path as he runs in.

- At the last moment, take a few steps back.

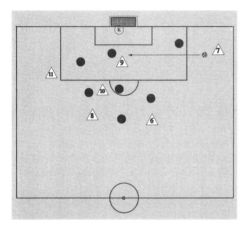
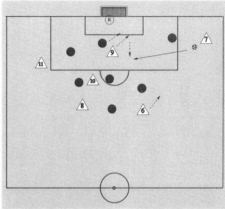

- The defender goes with the striker to the near post. At the last moment the striker takes a few steps back, so that he is free to receive the ball.

- It is important not to run past the near post.

- When an attacker runs in, he must start his sprint aggressively and then slow down slightly.

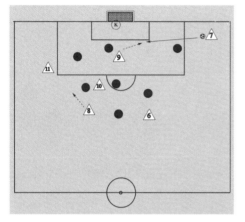

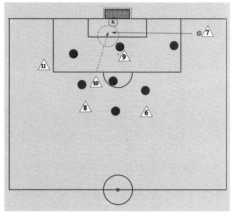

Sometimes it is hard to understand how goal-scoring chances can be missed. The cross is good, the attacker runs in with total conviction and heads the ball over an empty goal. Just before the ball arrives, the attacker should slow his run slightly and concentrate fully on heading the ball.

It is often difficult to score from wide of the near post.

- The player at the far post runs into the penalty area too soon.

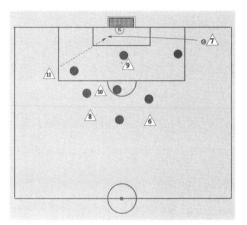

- When jumping to head the ball, it is important to take off on the foot furthest from the goal.

Cross from the right
Take off on the right foot

The player at the far post (often the winger) must leave sufficient space free before the ball is crossed. Often, however, he runs into the penalty area too soon. This increases the chance of an interception. If the cross is inaccurate, the player at the far post is often helpless. He is no longer able to adjust his position to the line of the ball. When the player at the far post is more patient and leaves more space, he can often reach the cross, even if it is inaccurate. It is easier to run in onto a cross than to adjust to the path of the ball from a standing position.

Cross from the left
Take off on the left foot

The attacker can head the ball more strongly if he takes off on the foot furthest from the goal.

Coaching ball skills

Coaching ball skills

Besides the aims of the game, we also devote attention to the individual technique of young soccer players. I am convinced that the coaching of ball skills has a place in youth soccer. The coaching of the skills needed to deceive an opponent and dribble past him brings added value to the learning process of young soccer players.

I view the coaching of ball skills more as fundamental support. Most of the practice sessions will be devoted to match-related drills (with the obstacles and constraints encountered in real matches, such as opponents, teammates, time, space and a defined playing area). I base my treatment of technical skills on real matches.

> By ball skills we mean changing direction and turning with the ball, faking, etc.

The main objectives of wing play are to create chances and supply crosses. Ball skills are subordinate to these objectives. Technique is the means with which these objectives are realized (by taking the ball past an opponent, playing an attacker into space, etc.). Attacking play down the flank requires more than dribbling tricks and fakes. Technical skill such as switching the play to the other flank and changing the direction of a run are frequently encountered in these drills.

The technical skills I deal with in this book are directly related to the aims of the wing play module. I have chosen simple, effective and realistic skills that can help the players to create chances. The most frequently occurring situations in wing play are:

- Opponent directly or diagonally in front of you.
- Opponent near you.
- Switching the play to the other flank.

The aims of wing play

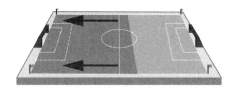

Aims:
- To create danger in the opposing team's penalty area.
- To score goals.

Means:
- Individual runs, combinations, forward passes, shots at goal.
- Crosses.

Conclusion with regard to ball skills:
Technical ball skills support these aims.

Switching the play to the other flank
The V movement

This movement can be used in the center of the field. The central defender (3) is challenged from one side by the opposing striker as he takes the ball forward. The defender drags the ball back and changes direction.

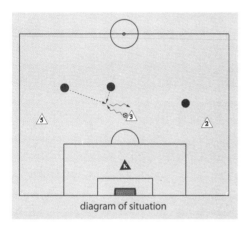

diagram of situation

photo of situation

Tips:
- If you make a short kicking movement with your right foot above the ball and also swing out your left arm, your opponent is more likely to be deceived.
- Change of rhythm after change of side.

Description of technique

Step 1: Place your foot on the ball.

Step 2: Drag the ball back under the sole of your foot.

Step 3: Push the ball in the other direction with the inside of the same foot.

Stepover and allow the ball to run through

This can be used to switch play to the other flank. The ball is played from the flank to the defensive midfielder (4). An opposing player is positioned to one side. The player allows the ball to run though. He then turns and plays the ball to the other flank.

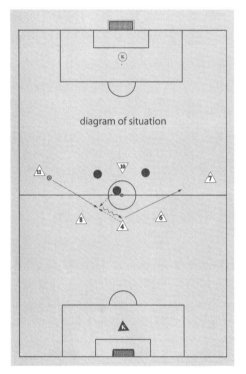

diagram of situation

photo of situation

Description of technique

Step 1: Step over the ball with your right foot from the outside inward and allow the ball to run between your feet.

Step 2: Turn quickly.

Tips:
- As you turn, make sure that the ball stays out of reach of the defender.
- If possible, cut across your opponent's path.

Turn with the ball, using the inside of your foot

Same situation. The player turns as he takes the ball.

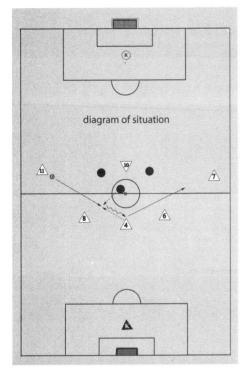

diagram of situation

photo of situation

Description of technique

Step 1: Place your left foot beside the ball and use the inside of your right foot to take the ball with you as you turn.

Step 2: Turn quickly.

Tips:

- As you turn, make sure that the ball stays out of reach of the defender.
- If possible, cut across your opponent's path.

Opponent beside you
Stop the ball and turn back

The right back (2) runs with the ball down the flank. An opponent is near him. When the opponent moves to challenge him, the right back stops the ball with his right foot, turns back and takes the ball with him using the outside of the left foot.

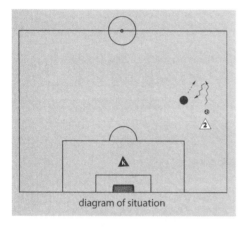

diagram of situation

photo of situation

Tips:
- Before the defender stops the ball, he can fake to cross the ball or play a forward pass (draw his foot back and extend his arm).
- If possible, cut across your opponent's path.
- Change of rhythm after turning back.

Description of technique

Step 1: Stop the ball with the sole of your right foot.

Step 2: Step over the ball with your right foot.

Step 3: Turn back and take the ball with you, using the outside of your left foot.

The Cruyff trick

The midfielder (6) makes a forward run with ball at his feet. As his opponent challenges for the ball, the midfielder turns away.

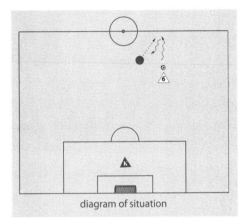

diagram of situation

photo of situation

Tips:
- Position yourself as though you are going to kick the ball (draw your foot back, raise your arm).

Description of technique

Step 1: Place your left foot ahead and to the left of the ball, then use the inside of your right foot to push the ball across the back of your left foot.

Step 2: Turn and take the ball with you.

Turn back using the outside of your foot

The left back (5) makes a run infield with the ball at his feet. As his opponent challenges for the ball, the full back turns away with the ball, using the outside of his right foot.

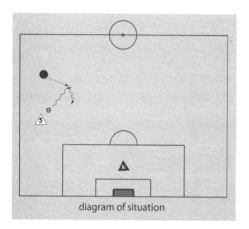

diagram of situation

Description of technique

Step 1: Keep your body between your opponent and the ball.

Step 2: Turn back with the ball, using the outside of your right foot.

photo of situation

Tip:

- Shield the ball with your body.

Stepover and turn back

The midfielder (8) makes a run with the ball at his feet. An opponent is on his left. As the opponent challenges for the ball, the midfielder turns away.

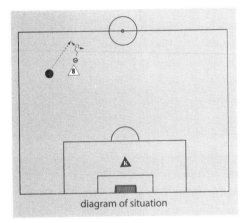

diagram of situation

photo of situation

Tips:
- Make the stepover in the direction of your opponent.
- Quickly turn and take the ball in the other direction.

Description of technique

Step 1: Place your left foot just ahead and to the left of the ball. Step over the ball with your right foot from outside to inside.

Step 2: Turn back and take the ball with you, using the inside of the left foot.

Opponent in front

Inside – outside

The ball is played to the winger on the flank.
He starts a run.

diagram of situation

photo of situation

Tips:
- Fake to go to the left.
- Knees slightly bent.

Description of technique
Step 1: Your left leg is your standing leg.
Step 2: Push the ball inside (to the left) with
the inside of your right foot.
Step 3: Immediately, without touching the
ground with your right foot, push the
ball in the other direction (back to the
right) with the outside of your right
foot.

Inside – stepover – outside

The ball is played to the winger on the flank.
He starts a run.

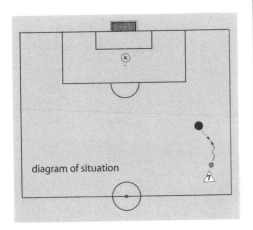

diagram of situation

photo of situation

Tips:
- Fake to go to the right.
- Knees slightly bent.

Description of technique

Step 1: Your left leg is your standing leg.

Step 2: Push the ball inside (to the left) with the inside of your right foot.

Step 3: Fake to take the ball in the other direction using the outside of the same foot, but step sideways over the ball.

Step 4: Take the ball on with the outside of the other foot.

Double scissor

The ball is played to the winger on the flank. He starts a run.

diagram of situation

1

photo of situation

2

Tips:
- Fake to go to one side then the other.
- Make the movement as quickly as possible
- Knees slightly bent

Description of technique
Step 1: Place your left foot beside the ball.
Step 2: Make a scissor movement (from the inside to the outside) round the ball with your right foot.
Step 3: Place your right foot beside the ball.
Step 4: Make a scissor movement (from the inside to the outside) round the ball with your left foot.
Step 5: Take the ball on with the outside of the right foot.

Stepover inside

The ball is played to the winger on the flank. He starts a run.

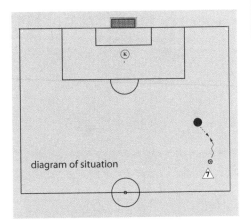

diagram of situation

photo of situation

Tips:
- Fake to go to one side then the other.
- Make the movement as quickly as possible
- Knees slightly bent

Description of technique

Step 1: Step over the ball with your right foot (from outside to inside).

Step 2: Take the ball on immediately with the outside of the same foot.

Scissor inside

The ball is played to the winger on the flank.
He starts a run.

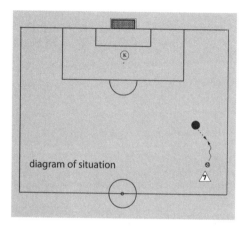

diagram of situation

photo of situation

Tips:
- Fake to go to inside.
- Make the movement as quickly as possible
- Knees slightly bent

Description of technique

Step 1: Make a scissor movement (from the inside to the outside) round the ball with your right foot.

Step 2: Take the ball toward the outside immediately with the outside of the right foot.

Scissor outside

The ball is played to the winger on the flank.
He starts a run.

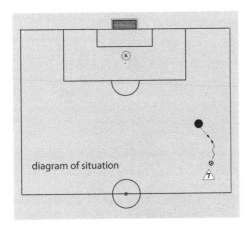

diagram of situation

photo of situation

Tips:
- This movement is ideal for making an inside run.
- Make the movement as quickly as possible
- Knees slightly bent

Description of technique

Step 1: Step over the ball with your right foot (from inside to outside).

Step 2: Take the ball toward the inside immediately with the inside of the same foot.

57

Stepover outside and intermediate step

The ball is played to the winger on the flank. He starts a run.

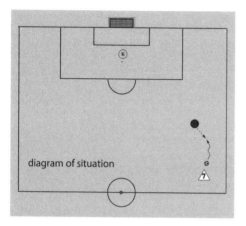

diagram of situation

photo of situation

Tips:
- Fake to go past your opponent on the left.
- Make the movement as quickly as possible.
- Knees slightly bent.

Description of technique
Step 1: Place your left foot beside the ball.
Step 2: Step over the ball with your right foot (from inside to outside).
Step 3: Take an intermediate step (fake) with your left foot.
Step 4: Take the ball on with the outside of the right foot.

Drag inside

The ball is played to the winger on the flank. He starts a run.

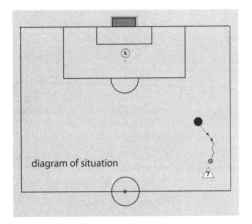

diagram of situation

photo of situation

Tips:
- This movement is ideal for making an inside run.
- Lean to the left.
- If your opponent blocks your path inside, you can take the ball to the outside with the outside of your right foot.
- Keep your foot in contact with the ball.
- Make the movement as quickly as possible.

Description of technique

Step 1: Place your left foot diagonally beside the ball.

Step 2: Drag the ball inside with the inside of the right foot.

59

Okocha movement

The ball is played to the winger on the flank. He starts a run.

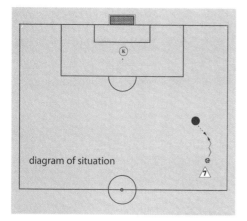

diagram of situation

photo of situation

Tips:
- Fake with your body.
- Step energetically over the ball to the inside.

Description of technique

Step 1: Place your left foot beside the ball.

Step 2: Use the sole of your right foot to roll the ball from outside to inside.

Step 3: Step over the ball with your left foot from outside to inside.

Step 4: Take the ball with the outside of the foot.

Fake to the outside and inside alternately

The ball is played to the winger on the flank. He starts a run.

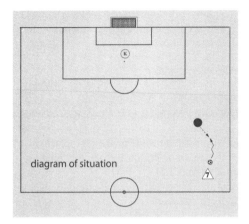

diagram of situation

photo of situation

Tips:
- Do this at speed.
- Fake with your body.
- You can tap the ball outside or inside several times before suddenly taking it in the opposite direction.
- You can combine this movement with stepovers, scissor, etc.
- Try to make your opponent lose his balance.

Description of technique
Step 1: Tap the ball inside using the inside of the foot.
Step 2: Tap the ball outside using the outside of the foot.

TRAINING FOR 1v1 SITUATIONS

In the flank module, the main focus is 1v1 situations. This is one of the most frequently occurring situations on the flank and is a very important stimulus for young players.

There are various ways of coaching for 1v1 situations. In practice, all sorts of drills are used to encourage players to dribble past their direct opponent. The chosen drills are not always very effective. In many cases they are not related to real game situations and the trick and fake movements are practiced for their own sake.

Each drill should have a certain return. The objective is to use drills that enable techniques to be applied in real game situations as quickly as possible. The coach has to take a number of factors into consideration. These factors have an influence on the content of the drills.

The objective is to use the movements in real game situations as quickly as possible.

The level of skill of the players
Young soccer players who have already acquired some level of skill will be able to start functional drills or practice drills with opponents sooner.

Age group
In the case of the younger players, more emphasis will be placed on the movements needed to dribble past an opponent. Individual drills will be used. Older groups will mainly carry out drills involving opponents.

Number of training sessions per week
The coach can focus more on the movements if there are 3 sessions per week than if there is only one.

The coach's background
In some cases the coach's background plays a role. A coach who was a skillful right winger will have a different approach to the movements needed to dribble past an opponent than a former defender.

The coach's skills
The coach's level of skill has a major influence on the coaching yield and the translation of ball skills into practice.

It is impossible to lay down a fixed pattern for coaching the application of the movements needed to dribble past an opponent in real games. The practical situation determines the steps to be taken.

Requirements for coaching ball skills and the 1v1 situation

- Ball skills and the 1v1 situation must be aligned to a position or a situation arising from a position.
- The coaching of ball skills must take account of the specific qualities of each individual player.
- Players must be encouraged to think about ball skills while learning how to improve them. Aspects such as "when", "how" and "where" are important.
- The place where the players practice the skill or 1v1 situation must bear a relationship to a real match situation.
- The players must play in the right direction.
- There must be a follow-up to the technical skill.
- The movement must be simple and efficient

I have divided the translation of 1v1 situations into real game situations into 5 steps. It is not the intention that the coach should go through these 5 phases. Depending on the needs of the group, the time available, the age of the players, and the coach's skills and background, the coach can choose from the following steps:

1. **Individual coaching of the movements needed to dribble past an opponent**
2. **Functional coaching of the movements needed to dribble past an opponent**
3. **1v1 with a "handicapped" defender**
4. **1v1**
5. **Translation of 1v1 into a match situation**

Step 1: Individual coaching

In the requirements for coaching ball skills, I mainly refer to functional coaching of the movements needed to dribble past an opponent. In view of the faster yield, these drills are preferred. Individual encouragement of players is an option if there is sufficient coaching time available. The aim of individual drills is to practice the technical and coordinative aspects of ball skills. Since no opponents or match situations are involved, the players are not distracted but can focus completely on the movement. The movement can be repeated dozens of times until it becomes second nature.

The aim is for the player to be able to carry out the movement perfectly. Unnecessary obstacles (complex drills, run lines and situations) must be avoided.

Unfortunately, individual coaching of the movements needed to dribble past an opponent is not always focused on technique alone. The drills are often too complex (difficult run lines and situations) and the techniques are not functional. The players are therefore occupied more with the organization, while the aim of the drill (practicing a technique or movement) fades into the background.

Individual drills must be as simple and realistic as possible. Simple drills with lots of repetition and functional movements take precedence. They are useful aids for learning how to repeat techniques faultlessly time after time. They can best be carried out at the start of a training session. When the coach sees that the players have mastered the techniques, he can switch to more functional drills.

Tips:
- Ensure that the movements are efficient and realistic.
- Carry out the movement step by step. Try to explain the movement in stages.
- Ensure first of all that the movement is

63

- The speed of execution of the movement can then be increased.
- Practice the movements on both sides of the field.
- Coach combinations of movements.
- Leave the players to themselves at first. Let them get on with it. Observe which players have which skills. Then try to broaden their range of skills.
- Do not try to do too much at once.
- It is fun to link a movement with a player's name, for example the "Peter trick."
- Try to encourage the players to practice movements regularly. The start of the training session (warming up) is the best time.
- Make sure that lots of repetitions are guaranteed.
- Choose simple organizational forms.
- Give the players homework.

Example of an individual drill:

I choose a drill in which the number of repetitions is guaranteed.

The players practice the following movements:

- Inside - outside
- The Okocha movement
- Stepover to the outside and intermediate step

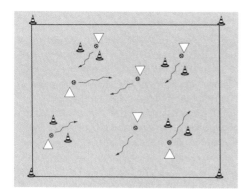

Organization:

a. The players all run freely with the ball. When they dribble it through a gate, they carry out a movement (movement to the right, then to the left).

b. The players are allowed two minutes to dribble the ball through as many gates as possible.

c. A defender is positioned in each gate. If the defender intercepts the ball, the players change roles.

Step 2: Functional coaching of ball skills

Functional coaching of ball skills is clearer for the players. The "recognition factor" is greater. The location on the field, the direction of play and the situation are closer to real matches. The players grasp more quickly how movements can be used in real match situations.

Tips:
- See the tips for individual drills.
- Ensure that the location on the field is appropriate. Players usually dribble past an opponent on the flank.
- Choose the right direction of play. Try to organize the drill so that it is carried out in the direction of the fixed goal. In some cases (larger groups, more repetitions), the drill can also be carried out in other directions.
- Take account of the positions of the (virtual) defenders. The defender is usually inside the winger.
- Ensure that the technique or movement is executed with the right attitude.
- Ensure that the drill can be developed into a 1v1 situation.
- Ensure that the follow-up corresponds to the location on the field. The winger's run will be followed by a cross or a shot at goal.
- The execution of the movement must serve the aims of the game. Taking the ball past an opponent must guarantee that a chance is created or a goal is scored.

Example of a functional drill:

The players practice the following movements:

- Inside - outside
- The Okocha movement
- Stepover to the outside and intermediate step

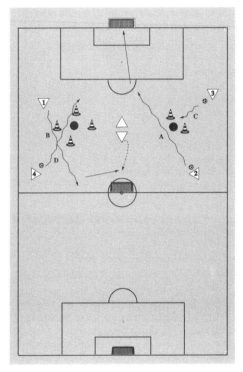

Organization:

Player 1 dribbles the ball to the cone, carries out a movement inside for taking the ball past an opponent and shoots. Players 2, 3 and 4 do the same in sequence.

Move through: Player 1 becomes player 4 – player 2 becomes player 3.

- Inside run – shoot (A)
- Outside run – cross (B)
- Left back (C)
- Zonal defender (D)

Step 3: 1v1 with a "handicapped" defender

A handicapped defender is a line defender, a zone defender or a defender with a disadvantage relative to his opponent (e.g. distance from his opponent). If the players can move directly from practicing a technique or movement to a 1v1 situation, this phase is unnecessary. A handicapped defender can always be introduced if the players are not very successful when they try out a newly acquired technique. Handicapping the defender gives the attacker a better chance of using a movement successfully. A handicapped defender is especially useful when players are practicing 1v1.

Tips:
- The resistance offered by the defender can be gradually increased.
- Ensure that the defender has a realistic chance of winning the ball.
- Ensure that the defender can score a goal if he wins the ball.
- The defender's position should be the same as his position in a real match.
- A handicapped defender can play in combination with a non-handicapped defender.
- Don't spend too long on this phase. Move on to 1v1 situations involving "real" defenders as soon as possible.

Examples of drills involving a handicapped defender:

The players practice the following movements:

- Stepover to the outside
- Double scissor
- The Okocha movement
- Stepover to the outside and intermediate step

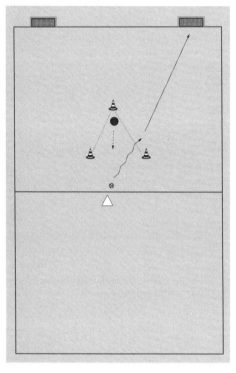

Organization:

- The player with the ball tries to dribble down one of the flanks.
- The defender tries to prevent him.
- If the defender wins the ball, the players changes places.
- The attacker can score in either of the two small goals.

Step 4: 1v1

Training for 1v1 situations is a core part of learning the movements needed to dribble past an opponent. When the functional aspects of the movements have been learned, the 1v1 situation is the most important follow-up step. The aim must always be to bring out the relevance to real match situations. The direction of play, the location on the field and the relationship to a situation on the field can put a movement or technique into the right context. The coach must find situations that are suitable for making things clear to the players.

Tips:
- Start from the winger's position or a real match situation.
- Ensure that the opposition can also score.
- Ensure a good work/rest balance.
- Ensure that the situation is on the flank.
- Pay attention to the direction of the play. The winger should play toward the fixed goal.
- Encourage players to be themselves. Encourage the players to try out their movements and fakes.
- Ensure that the defender's position corresponds to his position in a real match.
- Build up to 2v1 and 2v2 if possible.
- Encourage the players; coach positively.
- If the attackers dribble past the defenders too easily, the coach must encourage the defenders. The obstacles in the drills must correspond to obstacles encountered in real matches.

Examples of 1v1 drills:

The players practice the following movements:
- Stepover to the outside
- Double scissor
- The Okocha movement
- Stepover to the outside and intermediate step

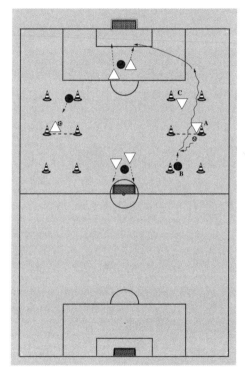

Organization:

- The winger (A) runs with the ball and tries to dribble past the defender. If he succeeds, he crosses the ball.
- If the defender (B) wins the ball, he can run with it into the other zone. He then tries to dribble past the defender (C).
- We continue until one of the players dribbles past his opponent and crosses the ball.
- When a player loses the ball, he takes the place of the defender.

In front of goal:
- Just two attackers
- Two attackers and one defender

Step 5: Application of skills in a match situation

The application of the movements needed to dribble past an opponent and 1v1 skills in match situations is often neglected. Unless they are used in match situations, however, they cannot be fully exploited. Placing movements or situations in a match context brings about a transfer of these skills. Movements can best be put into practice in small drills with lots of repetition. Match-related drills such as 3v3, 4v4 and 5v5 are ideal for coupling the technical aspect to insight. The tactical aspects come more to the fore in match-related drills involving more players (7v7, 8v8). In particular, the "where" and "when" aspects can be worked out. The content of the drills need not always be oriented toward the movements needed to dribble past an opponent. As indicated in the introduction, the movements are a means for achieving the aims of the game. The coach can offer advice about movements at appropriate moments during match-related drills.

Encouraging ball skills in match-related drills by means of:
- success moments
- tasks
- the organization of the drill

Practical examples:
Rewards
If a goal is scored after a cross, it counts double.

Task
The defenders are given the task of forcing the winger infield. The winger tries to dribble past the defender on the outside.

Organization
Make the field wider to give the winger a better chance of dribbling past the defender.

Tip:
- Making a run with the ball must not become an aim in itself.
- Avoid tasks that are too artificial
- Don't forget "free" play

Tips for coaching 1v1 situations

In view of the importance of being able to dribble past an opponent on the flank, I have divided the tips into 2 groups:

- Practicing movements
- Practicing 1v1 situations

Coaching movements for dribbling past an opponent

When coaching movements for dribbling past an opponent, it is important to start from the player's individual qualities. Each player has his own style of dribbling. When players are introduced to a drill, movement or situation, they should be given the time to discover what it is about. During this discovery phase (in which the players freely practice the movement), the coach has the time to analyze the players' individual qualities. He can then take these into consideration as the training session proceeds. It is also good if a coach uses players' successes to illustrate his talks or demonstrations.

Some tips:

Right attitude.
When players practice a movement, they do not always do so with the right attitude. The drills are often carried out sluggishly, with little variation in pace. In the first phase it is important for the players to acquire the necessary coordination to master a movement. It is pointless to ask them to speed up if they have not yet mastered the necessary technique.

When the players are in control of the ball, the intensity of the drill can be increased. This is the moment when the importance of a correct attitude should be emphasized. As their attitude changes and they become more determined, their technical skills come under more pressure. If the players carry out movements and techniques too sluggishly and with too little conviction, this will be reflected in match-related drills later.

tips:
- Increase the ball tempo – ensure that the (virtual) defender is put under pressure.
- Cultivate a winning mentality.
- Carry out movements with the necessary conviction.

Ensure that the first touch is good
Ball control is often a major obstacle in a real match. Pressure can also be exerted in simulated competitive situations. You often see players set off on a run from a stationary position. This rarely occurs in a real match. Confronting players with a variety of match-related passes (pass along the ground, pass through the air) forces them to develop their coordinative skills (receive with the first touch and go with the second touch).

- When you receive the ball, try to control it in such a way that you can go forward.
- Touch the ball frequently as you run with it, so that you can react quickly if an opponent challenges.
- Try to control the ball with your first touch so that you can play it in the direction you want with your second touch.

Be forceful
Increasing the speed of the drills forces the players to act faster. This stimulates their skills and brings their speed of action closer to the level needed in 1v1 situations. If the players are allowed to slow down the pace of the drills, this will be reflected in 1v1 situations.

The attacker dictates the tempo, not the defender (keep the defender under pressure).

Go directly toward the defender or draw him to the right or the left.

There are two ways to take the ball past an opponent:

Take the ball directly toward him.

Draw the defender inside and take the ball past him on the outside, or vice versa.

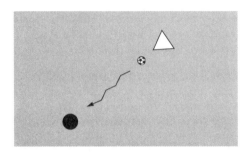

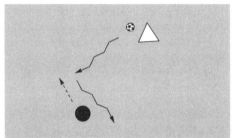

The choice is usually made on the basis of insight. The coach can, however, devote time to specific skills. The execution of typical techniques for passing an opponent on the inside or the outside is welcome at this stage.

Use your body to fake to the side.

Tips:
- Keep your knees slightly bent (lower center of gravity).
- The fake comes mainly from the upper half of your body.

Time the body swerve or fake or trick properly
It is important to learn when to carry out a movement. Ideally this should be practiced against a real defender, but a cone or a line or a gate can also be used to help players estimate distances.

Tips:
- Start the movement at a sufficient distance from the defender.
- Take the initiative or wait for a reaction from the defender.

Accelerate after dribbling past your opponent
The player's attitude is decisive here. If the player does not accelerate after dribbling the ball past a virtual defender, this will be reflected in 1v1 situations. After a player dribbles past a cone, he must accelerate.

What is the next step after going past an opponent?
Dribbling the ball past an opponent should not be an aim in itself. It must be done for a purpose. The player should know what he wants to do after leaving his opponent behind him.

Tips:
- Remain focused after dribbling past an opponent.
- Be aware of the situation around you.
- Run with the ball, shoot at goal, pass to a teammate, cross the ball.

Coaching 1v1 situations

Here, too, it is interesting to establish a framework. Again, it is important to start from the player's individual qualities. A coach can learn useful information simply by allowing the players to follow their inclination for a while. Some players have specific movements for taking the ball past an opponent. Other simply rely on speed. Each player's abilities must be analyzed. The coach can then decide what approach to take. A player who relies on speed will sooner or later come up against problems. By encouraging him to practice certain effective movements and giving him a better insight into 1v1 situations, the coach prepares him for the future.

Start from the player's individual qualities.

Right attitude
In a 1v1 situation, one player has to overcome the other. By approaching the situation with the right attitude, an attacker forces his opponent onto the defensive.

- Dare to take on the defender!
- Want to win!
- Don't be put off!

The first touch is important
Controlling the ball under pressure from an opponent is difficult. The position of the opponent influences the way the ball is controlled.

- Try to control the ball in such a way that you can go forward.
- Keep the ball away from your opponent.
- Touch the ball as often as you can, so that you can react quickly if your opponent challenges.

Dribbling past an opponent
Option 1: Put pressure on your opponent
Maintaining a fast pace puts pressure on an opponent. He therefore loses the initiative in a 1v1 situation.
- Maintain a fast pace. Make the defender move.
- The attacker dictates the pace, not the defender.

Option 2: Switch from slow to fast
Approach your opponent with the ball at your feet. A soon as your opponent slows his pace, make your move to go past him. The sudden switch from slow to fast catches the defender by surprise.

Go toward your opponent and draw him to the right or left
The player with the ball decides how to go past his opponent. Drawing an opponent to one side or the other is a question of insight. The skill level of the player is also a factor. Some players can dribble past a defender more easily on the inside, and some on the outside. The skill level of the defender is also an important aspect. Older players in particular must learn how to size up an opponent as part of their development.

- Drawing a defender:
Draw the defender in a given direction by taking the ball in that direction. The defender has to move to cover the attacker's path. As the defender moves, the attacker can take the ball past him in the other direction.

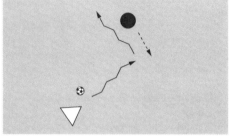

Draw your opponent to the outside and pass him on the inside.

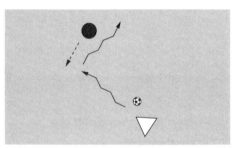

Draw your opponent inside and pass him on the outside.

- Approach the defender directly

There are two options:
a) Maintain a fast pace and make the defender move.
b) Suddenly switch from slow to fast.

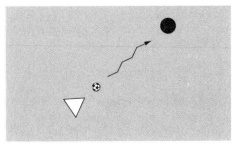

Use your body when you fake
Using the whole body to make a fake is above all an African/Brazilian specialty. A fake requires more than just leg movement. The upper body plays a key role in deceiving an opponent.

"The moment to take the ball past an opponent is when he goes into 'wait' mode."

Time the movement properly

The timing of the fake depends on a number of factors. The position on the field, the position of the opponent, the quality of the first touch when receiving the ball, whether the player is stationary or moving when he receives the ball, etc. Sometimes an attacker has very little time to make a movement. By practicing 1v1 challenges frequently, the attacker learns to estimate distances and to time his movements properly.

Accelerate after making a fake

In this early phase, players frequently lose possession. It is important to follow a fake with a decisive run. An appropriate movement and acceleration are essential in order to get past an opponent. In practice, players are often not fast enough to dribble past an opponent. The attacker frequently takes the ball too close to the defender, and as a result it is intercepted.

Cut across the line of the defender's run if possible

What happens after the ball is taken past the defender?

It is important that the player with the ball remains aware of the situation around him after he goes past an opponent. This situation makes a lot of demands on his insight and technique. Adapting the follow-up action (a cross or a shot at goal) to situations that occur in real matches improves the outcomes of 1v1 situations in such matches.

Making a run down the flank

Taking the ball past an opponent on the inside or the outside

Players should be confronted with key soccer situations when they practice the movements needed to dribble past an opponent in a 1v1 situation. In the case of wingers, they need to practice going past an opponent on the inside or the outside as often as possible.

- A run on the outside followed by a cross

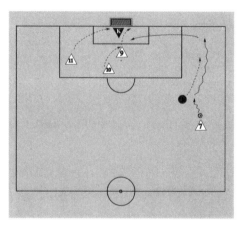

A run down the flank, taking the ball past an opponent on the outside, is one of the most attractive aspects of wing play. Many players are inclined to take the ball inside the defender. The coach should encourage his players to dribble past their opponent on the outside.

- A run inside followed by a shot at goal

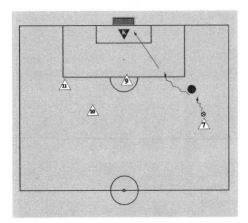

The way in which a winger dribbles past his opponent depends on the winger's strengths. If he is fast, he might prefer to take the ball past his opponent on the outside, where he has more space. A left-footer playing on the right flank might prefer to take the ball inside his opponent. By moving inside, he also creates options on the flank. For example, a midfielder or full back can make a forward run.

Making space for a 1v1 situation

When the ball is passed to the winger (7), his teammates must leave him enough space for the 1v1 situation.
- The striker (9) stays in the center in front of the goal.
- The midfielder (6) offers support, but stays at a sufficient distance. He does not take his marker with him toward the winger.

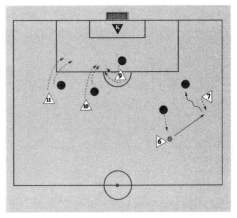

By taking the free defender with him at just the right moment, the striker (9) creates space for the winger (7) and creates a 1v1 situation for him.

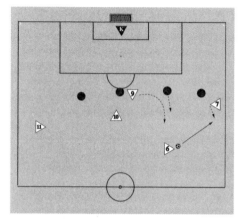

Where and when can a run be started?

15 to 18-year olds
The decision whether to try to take the ball past an opponent depends mainly on the position on the field. The risk is least when the midfielders and defenders are organized behind the winger (see Figure 1).

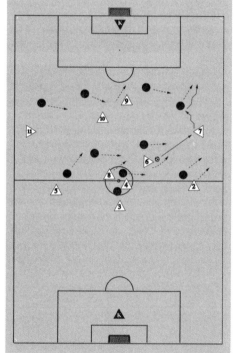

Figure 1

"You can try to dribble past an opponent in the opposition's half. In your own half, it is all about positional play."

Maarten Stekelenburg,
Ajax Amsterdam youth coach

If the defense is disorganized and therefore susceptible to a counterattack, there is a risk that losing possession in a 1v1 situation will give the opposition a chance to score (see Figure 2).

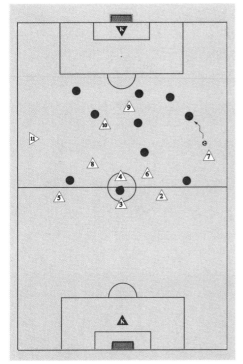

Figure 2

To create a 1v1 situation for a winger, good positional play and fast ball circulation are required. A winger in a 1v1 situation can make a run with the ball, but can best do this in the opposing team's half.

The winger must be able to assess whether a run is the best option in a 1v1 situation. The first touch when he receives the ball must be good. He should be facing his opponent when he receives the ball. If he has his back to him, the risk of losing possession is too great.

If the situation is less than ideal, e.g. if the pass to the winger is too hard or the ball bounces awkwardly, it is better not to take on the defender in a 1v1 situation. The winger must

be able to assess whether he can deal with any given 1v1 situation. In the case of older players, the end product of the run is the important factor. The "where" and "when" of the situation are also important.

None of this means that the winger cannot take any risks at all. He has sufficient space to be able to take a risk occasionally.

10 to 14 year-olds

Younger players are given more space in 1v1 situations. The product in a match situation is not relevant at this age. The soccer ability of the players is central. Loss of possession in not a problem. Taking the ball past several opponents stimulates the creative skills of the players.

> *Putting restrictions on dribbling past opponents stifles the development of young players.*

Practical example – different philosophies for different age groups

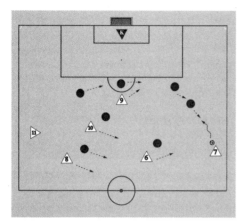

Philosophy for 15 to 18-year olds
The opposition exerts pressure on the flank where the ball is. The winger is outnumbered. Trying to run with the ball is too risky. There is space on the other flank. The ball is passed back and then across to the other flank. The left winger (11) can make a run with the ball.

Philosophy for 10 to 14-year olds
The winger can take on his opponent in a 1v1 situation. The coach allows the player to experiment. The coach also offers the player other options, e.g. a pass to a teammate, without detracting from the player's individual qualities or discouraging initiative.

> "If Kalou tries to take on an opponent 20 times and he fails every time, he can try again. But not in his own half, facing his own goal."
>
> *Bert van Marwijk*

COACHING METHOD
Coaching the aims of the game
and soccer problems

10 to 14-year olds

COACHING THE AIMS OF THE GAME

Tips

The players
10 to 12-year-olds: Due to the transition from 7v7 or 8v8 to 11v11, the players have to make different choices. In particular, the choice between making a run and involving other players is a major challenge, in view of the larger playing area. The players need a lot of space for runs with the ball. It is the coach's task to encourage the players to make the right choices.

13 and 14-year-olds: The phase of rapid growth must be taken into account in the coaching of 10 to 14-year-olds. Fast developers may be able to exploit their physical advantage and take the ball past their opponents on the basis of their superior strength rather than technique. The older the players become, the harder it is to overcome their opponent. They must be encouraged to acquire technical skills if they are to develop further.

> *Young players prefer to take the ball past an opponent on the same side as their strongest foot. Encourage them to try the other side.*

Training sessions
10 to 12-year-olds: The transition from 7v7 or 8v8 to 11v11 can be influenced perfectly during training sessions. In the first phase the coach can introduce positional training (drills from 1v1 to 5v5) or a passing and shooting drill, which can be built up to 1v1 or 2v1. etc. The coaching instructions are more technically oriented. In the second phase, drills with larger groups and 2 lines (e.g. the attackers with 2 wingers and the midfielders or defenders) can be introduced. Drills from 6v4 to 7v7 are useful here. Alongside technical aspects, the coach can impart insights in the drills with 2 lines, e.g. about how to deal with the problems presented by space, time, teammates and opponents. Competitive 8v8 drills can be used. To accelerate the process of familiarizing the players with 11v11, the coach can occasionally choose an 11v11 drill.

13 and 14-year-olds: 13 and 14-year-olds have no problems with drills involving 2 lines. They are able to understand the content of drills ranging from 6v4 to 8v7. The flank module can be structured in various ways for 13 and 14 year-olds.

- Passing and shooting drill/positional training – positional training - match-related drill
- Line drills with 2 lines – match-related drill

The coach can focus in detail on technical aspects requiring a greater action radius during the training sessions, e.g. crossing to the far post, switching the play from one flank to the other, playing forward passes. These techniques can be developed from the age of 13 or 14.

> *The players must be encouraged to practice 1v1 situations in each training session.*

The coach
The coach needs time to encourage the players to dare to try to dribble past an opponent on the flank. The coach's attitude is important. With players in this age group, encouragement has a greater impact than is generally thought. The message to be sent to the players is that it doesn't matter if they don't always succeed when they try to go past an opponent. The coach must not discourage the players!

10 to 12-year-olds: 10 to 12-year-olds form the youngest group to play 11v11. At this age the players have the most space to maneuver. The wingers have a lot of freedom to make runs with the ball. The coach gives the players sufficient space to experiment. The winger can try to dribble past several players or try out the most unlikely runs. The coach encourages the players to show initiative in 1v1 situations.

13 and 14-year-olds: At this age, runs by the winger are still important. However, the coach must gradually put forward other solutions. A winger must learn to assess what the team can gain from his run with the ball and be able to feel that he is participating in a team performance.

> "Napoleon neglected to attack via the flanks just once, and that was at Waterloo."
>
> Guy Roux,
> coach of Auxerre, France

13 and 14-year-olds have a wider action radius and are keen to experiment with this. Their technique, timing of forward passes and long crosses leave room for improvement at this age.

The match
At the start of the game the players often put the coach's instructions into practice. The winger stands facing infield to receive a pass, uses the correct foot to control it, etc. After a while there is a deterioration. This is logical. The influence of the coach on the training session gradually decreases as time goes by and the players fall back into old habits. The winger moves too far away from the flank, takes up the wrong position to receive the ball, etc.

10 to 12-year-olds: The move to the wider field has a number of consequences. In games of 11v11, the players initially stand at the same distance from each other as in a game of 7v7 or 8v8. They move too far away from the flank, or fall back too far when the team loses possession. The coach must explain how far apart they must stand, and how to create space.

13 and 14-year-olds: At this age the game starts to resemble a real game of soccer. The players have more stamina and a bigger action radius, and have more insight. Forward passes and switches from one flank to the other are used more often, although there is room for improvement. The coach should pay attention to maintaining a balance between short and long passes to the winger.

Aim

> The flank module for 10 to 14-year-olds
> Aim: To learn 11v11
> "Learning to cope with match-related obstacles"
> Own position – 2 lines

Drills:

Discovery phase

Passing and shooting drill
Ball skills drill
1v1 drill

Positional training	Line training, 2 lines
2 : 1 =>	5 : 4 =>
2 : 2 =>	5 : 5 =>
3 : 2 =>	6 : 4 =>
3 : 2 =>	6 : 5 =>
3 : 3 =>	6 : 6 =>
4 : 2 =>	7 : 5 =>
4 : 3 =>	7 : 6 =>
4 : 4 =>	7 : 7 =>
5 : 4 =>	8 : 7 =>

Training phase

Positional training	Line training, 2 lines
2 : 1 =>	5 : 4 =>
2 : 2 =>	5 : 5 =>
3 : 2 =>	6 : 4 =>
3 : 2 =>	6 : 5 =>
3 : 3 =>	6 : 6 =>
4 : 2 =>	7 : 5 =>
4 : 3 =>	7 : 6 =>
4 : 4 =>	7 : 7 =>
5 : 4 =>	8 : 7 =>

Game phase

Match-related drill (8v8 or 11v11)

Practical example:
Learning one of the aims of the game

Young players do not have much insight when they play 11v11. They need to develop further before they can play in a 1-3-4-3 formation. We therefore speak of learning one of the aims of the game in this age group. The players learn the principles of one of the aims of the game. The example here is intended for players who have not yet mastered the basic principles of playing on the flank in an 11v11 game.

Learning one of the aims of the game

We have chosen the following sequence for the players to learn one of the aims of the game.

We determine:

The starting situation
 The age group
 The level
 The number of training sessions per week
 The starting level of the players

The development objective
 What do we want to achieve?

We then choose the following steps:

1. What playing system are we going to choose?
2. Which module do we want to choose?
3. Which players are we looking at?
4. Which part of the field and in which direction?
5. What drills should we choose?
6. How should we factor in the age-typical aspects?
7. How should we draw up the schedule?
8. What should be the content of the training session?

We determine
The starting situation:

Age group: 13 and 14-year-olds
Level: Higher amateur level
Number of training sessions per week: 2
Starting level of the players:
The players are familiar with the principles of play on the flank. They have played 11v11 for a number of years.

The development objective:
Creating chances via the flank
1v1 variations on the flank
Crossing; taking up positions in front of the goal

1. What playing system are we going to choose?
The players in this age group play in a 1-3-4-3 formation.

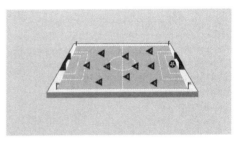

2. Which module do we want to choose?
The flank module.

3. Which players are we looking at?

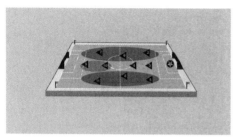

Primarily the wingers (7 and 11), the right and left midfielders (6 and 8) and perhaps the right and left backs (2 and 5), in cooperation with the striker (9) and the withdrawn striker (10).

4. Which part of the field and in which direction?

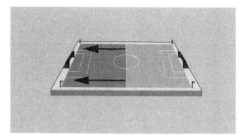

In the opposing team's half, in the direction of the opposing team's goal.

5. What drills should we choose?

- Passing and shooting drills.
- Ball skill drills
- 1v1 drills
- Positional training (from 2v1 to 5v5).
- Line training with 2 lines (from 5v5 to 8v8).

Passing and shooting drills are useful for focusing on technical aspects (e.g. crossing the ball). Ball skill drills are useful for introducing fakes and movements for taking the ball past an opponent. 1v1 drills are good for practicing situations on the flank. Positional training guarantees lots of repetitions. Drills with 2 lines improve the players' insight.

6. How should we factor in the age-typical aspects?

The 10 to 14 age group is in the learning phase for 11v11. Besides developing general skills, it is important to put the players more or less in their own positions. The players have more insight, so drills in which they have to overcome more difficulties (e.g. more players) are feasible. 13 and 14-year-olds are stronger, and this has a positive influence on practicing crosses and long passes.

7. How should we draw up the schedule?

This schedule is simply an example. Coaches should not merely copy it. Factors such as enthusiasm, form on the day, the translation of the aim of the game in practice and the time of year all influence the scheduling of the training sessions. Coaches must translate the aim of the game into practice in ways that suit their own situation.

Wednesday	**training**	**tactical**	**flank module**	**session 1**
Friday	training	technical/passing and shooting/ positional play/match-related drill		
Saturday	match			
Wednesday	**training**	**tactical**	**flank module**	**session 2**
Friday	**training**	tournament drill (4v4)		
Saturday	match			
Wednesday	**training**	**tactical**	**flank module**	**session 3**
Friday	**training**	**tactical**	**flank module**	**session 4**
Saturday	match			
Wednesday	training	finishing drills/positional play/match-related drill		
Friday	**training**	**tactical**	**flank module**	**session 5**
Saturday	match			
Wednesday	**training**	**tactical**	**flank module**	**session 6**
Friday	training	positional play/soccer tennis tournament		
Saturday	match			
Wednesday	**training**	**tactical**	**flank module**	**session 7**
Friday	training	technique/tag game/passing and shooting/ postitional play		
Saturday	match			

8. What should be the content of the training session?

The development objectives of the sessions.

Session 1: We start in the discovery phase with a passing and shooting drill with fakes and dribbling movements and 1v1 drills. In the training phase we couple technique to insight. The positional drill with 5v3 + goal-keeper is intended to create 1v1 situations. We finish the session with a match-related drill of 8v8.

In **session 2**, we expand the passing and shooting drill by involving a midfielder. In the training phase we offer the players a drill with 2 lines. The players learn how to play the winger into space, and when a winger can take on an opponent. We finish with a match-related drill.

Session 3: In the discovery phase we repeat the positional drill, but increase the level of difficulty. In the training with 2 lines we go a little further by introducing an opponent. We finish the session with a match-related drill.

Session 4 takes the line drill with 2 lines still further. The success moment from the previous session is repeated. In the training phase we extend this drill again. The players are ready for the next step. All the wingers are now involved in the drill. The variations on the flank are examined. In the match-related drill we play 8v8.

In **session 5** we repeat the passing and shoot-ing drill. Some of the variations on the flank are repeated. In the training phase we put these variations into practice. In the 8 + goal-keeper v 6 + goalkeeper drill the players try to play the winger into space.

Session 6 starts with a 3v2 drill on the flank. The 3-player team tries to win the ball from the other team and then to get the ball in front of the goal and score. They can make use of a number of variations. These variations can be tried out again in the training phase. The session ends with a match-related drill.

Session 1

Development objective of the session

Session 1: We start in the discovery phase with a passing and shooting drill with fakes and dribbling movements and 1v1 drills. In the training phase we couple technique to insight. The positional drill with 5v3 + goalkeeper is intended to create 1v1 situations. We finish the session with a match-related drill of 8v8.

Discovery phase:	Passing and shooting drill with faking and dribbling movements and 1v1
Training phase:	Positional training (5v3 + goalkeeper)
Game phase:	Match-related drill (8v8, depending on the number of available players)

Content of the session

Discovery phase:

Passing and shooting drill with faking and dribbling movements and 1v1

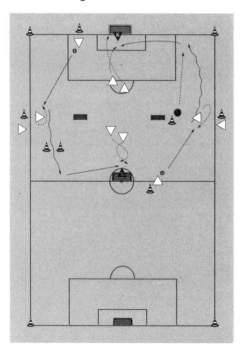

Organization:

- Start on both flanks at the same time.
- After x crosses, the players change flanks.
- Faking and dribbling movements at a gate formed by 2 cones.
- 1v1 with incoming defender (the defender sets off when the winger receives the ball).

We then start on the other flank.
The players either change positions (A goes to B, B to C, C to D and D to A) or stay in their fixed positions.

Coaching points:

- Do not run into the penalty area too soon.
- Have the right attitude: expect to score.
- Be first to the rebound.

Training phase: positional play 5v3+K

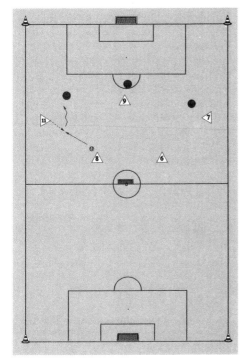

Organization:

- Task: Bring the winger into a 1v1 situation as often as possible.
- Success moment: If both wingers dribble past their opponent and cross to a team-mate twice, the attackers win. If the defenders score 3 times, the defenders win. The points scored by the attackers (e.g. by shooting into the goal) are subtracted from the defenders' total. Who wins?

Coaching points:

Winger
- Take care to choose the right moment.
- Make sure you are in the right position for a 1v1 situation.

Midfielders
- Cover the winger's run.
- Try to get the ball to the winger as quickly as possible.

Attackers in front of goal
- Score
- Be first to the rebound.

Game phase:

8v8 (depending on the number of available players).
Free play.

Session 2
Development objective of the session
In session 2, we expand the passing and shooting drill by involving a midfielder. In the training phase we offer the players a drill with 2 lines. The players learn how to play the winger into space, and when a winger can take on an opponent. We finish with a match-related drill.

Discovery phase:	Passing and shooting drill with variations and 1v1
Training phase:	Line training with 2 lines (6 + K v 4 + K)
Game phase:	Match-related drill (8v8, depending on the number of available players)

Content of the session
Discovery phase:
Passing and shooting drill with variations and 1v1

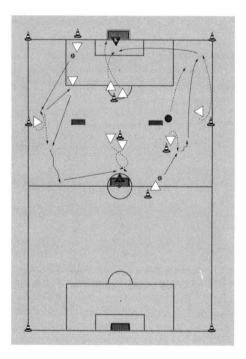

Organization:
- Start on both flanks at the same time.
- After x crosses, the players change flanks.
- The player with the ball passes to the midfielder, who passes the ball forward to the winger.
- The player with the ball passes to the winger, who passes it back to the midfielder; the midfielder passes the ball forward to the winger.
- 1v1 with incoming defender (the defender sets off when the winger receives the ball).

Coaching points:
Winger
- Do not make your forward run too soon.
- Keep running.
- If there is no defender, push the ball firmly forward as you run.
- Have a plan for taking the ball past the defender.
- Have a plan for 1v1 situations.

Attackers in front of goal
- Do not run into the penalty area too soon.
- Have the right attitude
- Score.
- Be first to the rebound.

Training phase:
Line training with 2 lines (6 + K v 4 + K)

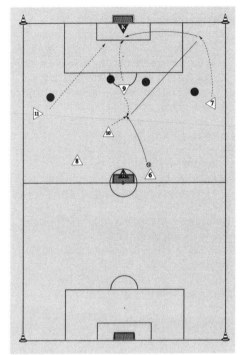

Organization:
Task of defenders (without telling the attackers): Exert pressure on the flank as quickly as possible.

Coaching points:
Winger
- 1v1 situation – make a run with the ball.
- Outnumbered – pass the ball back or square.
- Observe who is in front of the ball.
  - If the goalkeeper is at the near post, cross to the far post.

Midfielders
- Try to switch the ball to the other flank if necessary.

Attackers
- One attacker at the near post.
- One attacker at the far post
- The strikers' runs should cross in front of goal.

Game phase:
8v8 (depending on the number of available players).
Task for the 2 full backs: Force the winger toward the flank.

Session 3
Development objective of the session
Session 3: In the discovery phase we repeat the positional drill, but increase the level of difficulty. In the training with 2 lines we go a little further by introducing an opponent. We finish the session with a match-related drill.

Discovery phase:	Positional training (5v4 + K)
Training phase:	Line training with 2 lines (6 + K v 5 + K)
Game phase:	Match-related drill (8v8, depending on the number of available players)

Content of the session
Discovery phase:
Positional training (5v4 + K)

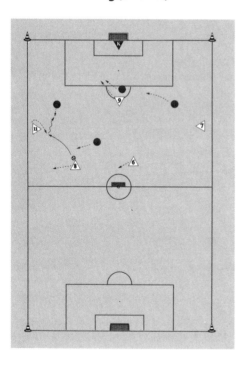

Organization:
- Task: Bring the winger into a 1v1 situation as often as possible.
- Success moment: If both wingers dribble past their opponent and cross to a team-mate 4 times, the attackers win. If the defenders score 3 times, the defenders win. The points scored by the attackers (e.g. by shooting into the goal) are subtracted from the defenders' total. Who wins?

Coaching points:
Winger
- Take care to choose the right moment.
- Make sure you are in the right position for a 1v1 situation.

Midfielders
- Cover the winger's run.
- Try to get the ball to the winger as quickly as possible.

Attackers in front of goal
- Score
- Be first to the rebound.

Training phase:
Line training with 2 lines (6 + K v 5 + K)

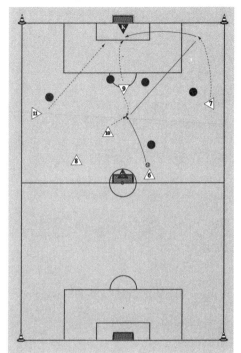

Organization:

Task of defenders (without telling the attackers):
Exert pressure on the flank as quickly as possible. The attackers try to anticipate this.

Coaching points:

General
- Circulate the ball quickly.
- Speed of the ball.

Wingers
- 1v1 situation – make a run with the ball.
- Outnumbered – pass the ball back or square.

Midfielders
- Try to switch the ball to the other flank as quickly as possible.

Attackers
- One attacker at the near post.
- One attacker at the far post
- The strikers' runs should cross in front of goal.

Game phase:

8v8 (depending on the number of available players).
Task: On two thirds of a full pitch. The wingers' team tries to create space behind the attackers by circulating the ball in and around the penalty area for a longer period.

Session 4

Development objective of the session

Session 4 takes the line drill with 2 lines still further. The success moment from the previous session is repeated. In the training phase we extend this drill again. The players are ready for the next step. All the wingers are now involved in the drill. The variations on the flank are examined. In the match-related drill we play 8v8.

Discovery phase: Line training with 2 lines (6v5 + K)

Training phase: Line training with 2 lines (8 + K v 6 + K)

Game phase: Match-related drill (8v8, depending on the number of available players)

Content of the session
Discovery phase:
Line training with 2 lines (6v5 + K)

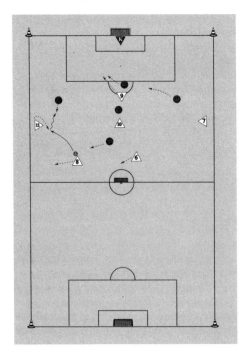

Organization:

- *Task:* Bring the winger into a 1v1 situation as often as possible.
- *Success moment:* The same as in the previous session Who wins now?

Coaching points:

Winger
- Take care to choose the right moment.
- Make sure you are in the right position for a 1v1 situation.

Midfielders
- Cover the winger's run.
- Try to get the ball to the winger as quickly as possible.

Attackers in front of goal
- Score
- Be first to the rebound.

Training phase:
Line training with 2 lines (8 + K v 6 + K)

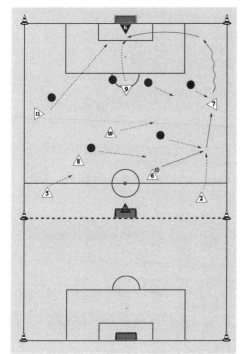

Organization:

Coaching points:
General
- How can we involve the midfielders and defenders in the play on the flank?
- What variations can be used to enable the winger to cross the ball?

Wingers
- 1v1 situation – make a run with the ball.
- Outnumbered – pass the ball back or square.
- When must we create space for other players?

Midfielders
- Try to switch the ball to the other flank as quickly as possible.
- Watch for players making a forward run.

Attackers
- Do not get too far apart.
- Keep moving

Game phase:
8v8 (depending on the number of available players).
Task: The defending team plays very defensively and waits for opportunities to counterattack.

Session 5
Development objective of the session
In session 5 we repeat the passing and shooting drill. Some of the variations on the flank are repeated. In the training phase we put these variations into practice. In the 8 + goalkeeper v 6 + goalkeeper drill the players try to play the winger into space.

Discovery phase: Passing and shooting drill
                               with variations and 1v1
Training phase: Line training with 3 lines
                               (8 + K v 6 + K)
Game phase: Match-related drill (8v8,
                               depending on the number
                               of available players)

Content of the session
Discovery phase:
Passing and shooting drill with variations / 2v1 and 2v2 in front of goal.

Organization:
- Start on both flanks at the same time.
- After x crosses, the players change flanks.

Variations:
- Pass to midfielder, pass to winger, get behind the defender.
- Pass to winger, pass back to midfielder, get behind the defender.
- The winger has the ball and moves infield while the midfielder moves out to the flank behind him.
- The players make their own choice (they must communicate).
- 2v1 – 2v2 in front of goal (defenders can score in the small goal).

Success moment:
The players must score 5 goals in x minutes.

Coaching points:
Winger
- Create space for the player who is making a forward run.
- Create space at the right moment.

Midfielders
- Play the ball far enough forward.
- Make sure the player making the forward run does not have to slow the pace of his run.

Training phase:
Line training with 3 lines (8 + K v 6 + K)

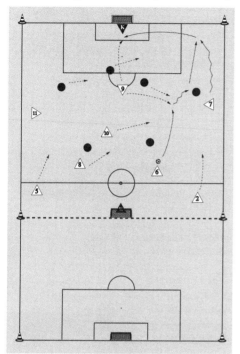

Organization:

Coaching points:
General
- When should a player take on an opponent in a 1v1 situation and when not?
- How can we involve the midfielders and defenders in the play on the flank?
- What variations can be used to enable the winger to cross the ball?

Wingers
- 1v1 situation – make a run with the ball.
- Outnumbered – pass the ball back or square.
- When must we create space for other players?

Midfielders
- Try to switch the ball to the other flank as quickly as possible.
- Watch for players making a forward run.

Attackers
- Do not get too far apart.
- Keep moving

Game phase:
8v8 (depending on the number of available players).
Task: The defending team plays very defensively and waits for opportunities to counter-attack.

99

Session 6
Development objective of the session
Session 6 starts with a 3v2 drill on the flank. The 3-player team tries to win the ball from the other team and then to get the ball in front of the goal and score. They can make use of a number of variations. These variations can be tried out again in the training phase. The session ends with a match-related drill.

Discovery phase: 3v2 on the flank and 2v1 in front of goal.

Training phase: Line training with 3 lines (8 + K v 7 + K)

Game phase: Match-related drill (8v8, depending on the number of available players)

Content of the session
Discovery phase:
3v2 on the flank and 2v1 in front of goal.

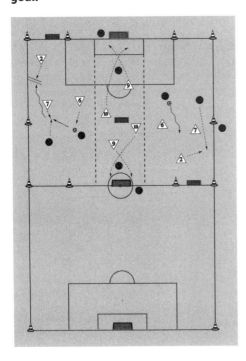

Organization:
- Start on both flanks at the same time.
- This drill incorporates a change of possession.
- The defenders have the ball and try to score in the small goal (the attackers outnumber the defenders by 3 to 2)
- The attackers try to win the ball and then cross it
- There is a 2v1 situation in front of goal and then a 2v2 situation.

Variations:
- When the defenders lose the ball they do not defend.
- When the defenders lose the ball they defend.

Success moment:
Who wins after 10 attempts by the attackers?

Coaching points:
General
- The offside rule applies.

Winger
- Try not to lose the ball easily.
- Make use of the space created.

Midfielders
- Play the ball forward immediately or play it square or back?

Defender
- Make an overlapping run down the flank or not?

Training phase:
Line training with 3 lines (8 + K v 7 + K)

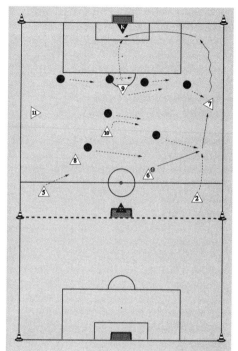

Organization:

Coaching points:
General
- When should a player take on an opponent in a 1v1 situation and when not?
- How can we involve the midfielders and defenders in the play on the flank?
- What variations can be used to enable the winger to cross the ball?

Wingers
- 1v1 situation – make a run with the ball.
- Outnumbered – pass the ball back or square.
- When must we create space for other players?

Midfielders
- Try to switch the ball to the other flank as quickly as possible.
- Watch for players making a forward run.

Attackers
- Do not get too far apart.
- Keep moving

Game phase:
8v8 (depending on the number of available players).
Free play.

Evaluation

Coaching the aims of the game

- **Do the players enjoy themselves?**
  There is sufficient variation in the drills
  (match-related drills, finishing).

- **Is the development objective achieved?**
  The players' performance in real matches
  demonstrates that they have been influenced. The players show more initiative on
  the flank. Clear progress has been made in
  the development objectives:
  - The creation of chances via the flank
  - The variations of 1v1 on the flank
  - The cross and the positions in front of goal

- **Is the number of practice drills in the
  training sessions limited?**
  There are a maximum of 3 drills in each
  training session.

- **Is the number of practice drills in the
  module limited?**
  A total of 5 practice drills are integrated in
  the module. All other drills are derived from
  these primary drills.

- **Is there a good balance between match-
  related and non-match-related drills?**
  The match-related drills dominate. The
  non-match-related drills such as passing and
  shooting drills with finishing are more
  supportive in nature.

- **Is there a progressive buildup over a
  certain period?**
  Six training sessions are completed over a
  period of 6 weeks. The level of difficulty of
  the drills is gradually increased.

- **Are there sufficient repetitions for the
  players?**
  All players are sufficiently involved in each
  drill.

- **Is sufficient consideration given to the
  age group of the players?**
  The drills used in these practical examples
  are oriented to the players' age group. The
  content is adjusted to the age of the players.

- **Are the drills adjusted to their level?**
  The drills are applicable at the higher
  regional level. If they are too difficult, the
  coach can easily adjust them.

- **Do the players have sufficient freedom of
  movement?**
  Sufficient free moments are incorporated.

14 to 18-year olds

PROBLEM ORIENTED COACHING

Tips

The players

The players in this age group have a good insight. The way in which they deal with the flank module is very mature. Their greater physical and technical abilities, allied to their insight, ensure that the wingers and wing play variations can be taken a long way forward. Analysis of strengths and weaknesses plays a major role here. A winger who is repeatedly unable to go past his opponent must find a solution to this problem. At this age, team performance is increasingly important, and if the winger cannot solve this problem he reduces the efficiency of the team as a whole. This does not mean that there is no longer room for experiment and creativity. However, the winger must choose his moment more carefully and be more aware of the strengths of his immediate opponent, the opposing team and his own team, and the players form on the day.

14 to 16-year-olds: At this age, the players are marked more closely. Wingers have less space than in younger age groups. The opposing players are stronger and offer more resistance when a winger tries to make a run with the ball. The winger has to make more choices to ensure that he remains just as productive despite the increased resistance. In particular, it is more difficult to remain calm in possession.

17 and 18-year-olds: This age group handles the flank module in a more balanced manner. The more hectic traits of the younger age group have been banished. The players are more self-assured and able to adjust to the strengths and weaknesses of the opposition. At this age, a player can assess how a match is going and whether he is in form.

> At this age, the focus is more and more on the winger's specific qualities.

Training sessions

In principle, players in this age group are able to handle line training with 3 lines. Position training and line training with 2 lines also help the winger to develop. Training sessions can be based on the types of resistance encountered in real matches. Specific work items from matches can be incorporated in the sessions. The players are ready for all types of flank variations.

14 to 16 year olds: The content of the training sessions is closer to that of adult soccer. No expectations are placed on younger players, but at this age a winger is expected to have a more serious attitude. The winger must integrate himself into the team play. From this age on there is more emphasis of passing and shooting, all types of crosses and heading at goal. The players are stronger, so the importance of fast ball circulation can be emphasized. There are more 1v1 challenges at this age. The players enjoy practicing how to escape from an opponent, and all that this involves.

17 and 18 year-olds: High expectations are placed on 17 and 18 year-olds. This is understandable, as the players are almost at the end of the soccer education process. All facets of soccer can be included in training sessions. The winger is often given specific tasks (depending on the coach's analysis of the strengths and weaknesses of the team and the opposition) in preparation for a match. The development of the individual must not be neglected within this collective tactical approach. Wingers still have lots of opportunities to develop their own way of playing.

The coach

> Training sessions can be based on the obstacles presented by the opposition.

The objectives of this age group, which increasingly regards winning as its main aim, must not be a hindrance to the players' development. The coach must be able to explain the role of the opposition clearly. For the winger, this means that creativity is still a top priority in the 14 to 18 age group. At the same time the coach must explain how the winger can contribute most effectively to the team. Too much attention to fixed run lines, flank variations and complicated tasks can kill creativity. Encourage the players and offer other solutions!

14 to 16 year-olds: Correct translation of a strengths and weaknesses analysis of the opposition requires a lot of talks and instruction from the coach. Regular comparisons of the efficiency of the winger's runs, the strengths of his opponent and his own work items help the winger to assess his own performance level.

17 and 18 year olds: High demands can be made of the players in this final phase. A winger must be able to perform well in each training session.

The match

> "The aim is to channel the capabilities of the players into a role and to compensate for or camouflage their weaknesses."
>
> *Aimé Antheunis*

The role of the winger may have to be adapted to the style of play of the opposition. When the opposing team plays 1 on 1 at the back, this requires a different approach than when it plays with a reinforced 5-man defense. The coach explains how to cope with the style of play beforehand. He discusses the various options and then it is up to the team. This is an independent process. The coach encourages during the match but keeps his distance. During half-time and after the match the developments are evaluated. In this way the winger learns independently, week by week, how to cope with different situations.

14 to 16-year-olds: Increased pressure on the ball and the limited space make life increasingly difficult for the winger. At this age, the most space is available just after winning possession.

17 and 18-year olds: The winger demonstrates maturity and self-assurance in his play. The players are able to take a tactical approach and demonstrate initiative during a match. Openings on the flank depend increasingly on the winger's skill, as the opposition is usually very well organized.

107

Aim

The flank module between 14 and 18

Aim:
- *To perfect playing 11v11*
- *To learn how to deal with the manner in which the opposition plays*
- *Collective development with regard to*
  - *the strengths and weaknesses of the players' own team and the opposition*
  - *the players' own positions, the line, the total team*

Drills for the discovery phase

Passing and shooting Ball skills 1v1	Positional training	Line training 2 lines	Line training 3 lines
	2 : 1 =>		
	2 : 2 =>	5 : 4 =>	8 : 6 =>
	3 : 2 =>	5 : 5 =>	8 : 7 =>
	3 : 3 =>	6 : 4 =>	8 : 8 =>
	4 : 3 =>	6 : 5 =>	9 : 6 =>
	4 : 4 =>	6 : 6 =>	9 : 7 =>
	5 : 4 =>	7 : 5 =>	9 : 8 =>
		7 : 6 =>	9 : 9 =>
		7 : 7 =>	10 : 8 =>
		8 : 7 =>	10 : 9 =>
			10 : 10 =>
			11 : 10 =>

Training phase

Line training 2 lines	Line training 3 lines
5 : 4 =>	8 : 6 =>
5 : 5 =>	8 : 7 =>
6 : 4 =>	8 : 8 =>
6 : 5 =>	9 : 6 =>
6 : 6 =>	9 : 7 =>
7 : 5 =>	9 : 8 =>
7 : 6 =>	9 : 9 =>
7 : 7 =>	10 : 8 =>
8 : 7 =>	10 : 9 =>
	10 : 10 =>
	11 : 10 =>

Game phase

Match-related drills (8v8 to 11 v11, depending on number of available players)

Practical example
Problem-oriented coaching
As the players get older, we talk of "problem-oriented coaching". The players have played 11v11 for a number of years and have built up a basic knowledge of the manner of playing. The coach can therefore base his coaching more on real match situations. The players know the aims of the flank play and the coach can treat them in more detail. If the players in this age group are not sufficiently advanced, the coach can focus on coaching the aims of the game (see example for 10 to 14 year-olds).

Problem-oriented coaching

Problem-oriented coaching involves the following steps.

First we determine:
- The starting situation
- The age group
- The level
- The number of training sessions per week
- The starting level of the players
- The soccer problem – who, what, where, when?
- The development objective – what do we want to achieve?

We then choose the following steps:
1. What playing system are we going to choose?
2. Which module do we want to choose?
3. Which players are we looking at?
4. Which part of the field and in which direction?
5. What drills should we choose?
6. How should we factor in the age-typical aspects?
7. How should we draw up the schedule?
8. What should be the content of the training session?

We determine
The starting situation:

Age group: 17 year olds
Level: Highest youth level
Number of training sessions per week: 3
Starting level of the players: The players know the aims of the flank play.

Soccer problem
When the team is in possession in the opposition's half, it takes too long for the ball to be played to the wingers. The ball stays too long on one flank and the players do not look for space by switching the play to the other flank.

The development objective
Switching the play to the other flank.

1. What playing system are we going to choose?
The players are familiar with a 1-4-3-3 formation.

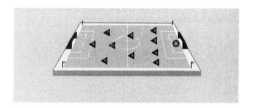

2. Which module do we want to choose?
The flank module.

3. Which players are we looking at?
Mainly the wingers, the midfielders, the striker and the withdrawn striker.

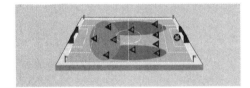

4. Which part of the field and in which direction?
In the opposition's half. We play from the center line in the direction of the fixed goal.

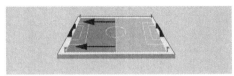

5. What drills should we choose?
The following drills can be used for the 14 to 18-year-old age group:
- Passing and shooting drills.
- Positional training (from 2v1 to 5v5).
- Line training with 2 lines (from 5v5 to 8v8).
- Line training with 3 lines (from 8v7 to 11v11).

Problem-oriented coaching mainly makes use of match-related drills.

6. How should we factor in the age-typical aspects?
In the oldest age group, the emphasis is on specialization in the player's own position. The positions that a player occupies during training sessions corresponds as far as possible to his strongest position.

7. How should we draw up the schedule?
This schedule is fictional. In practice, the details of the soccer conditioning would be included.

Saturday – The match
In the match, the coach is confronted with the
following soccer problem:
When the team is in possession in the opposition's half, it takes too long for the ball to be
played to the wingers. The ball stays too long
on one flank and the players do not look for
space by switching the play to the other flank.

Monday	**training**	**tactical**	**flank play**	**session 1**
Tuesday	training	conditioning		
Wednesday	training	Passing and shooting/positional play/game drill		
Thursday	**training**	**tactical**	**flank play**	**session 2**
Saturday	*match*	When the play is switched from one flank to the other, the striker (9) and withdrawn striker (10) are not sufficiently involved. This means that the opposition can reorganize too easily.		
Monday	**training**	**tactical**	**flank play**	**session 3**
Tuesday	training	conditioning		
Wednesday	training	Passing and shooting/positional play/game drill		
Thursday	**training**	**tactical**	**flank play**	**session 4**
Saturday	match	The players switch the play smoothly from one flank to the other.		
Monday	training	soccer tennis tournament		
Tuesday	training	conditioning		
Wednesday	training	Passing and shooting/positional play/game drill		
Thursday	**training**	**tactical**	**flank play**	**session 5**
Saturday	match	The players again switch the play smoothly from one flank to the other.		

8. What should be the content of the training session?

The development objectives of the training sessions.

In **session 1** we start with a passing and shooting drill, with the focus on technical aspects (for switching the play from one flank to the other). In this drill, we work with specific positions from a real match. In the training phase we move to a drill with 2 lines (6v5 + goalkeeper). This combines technique and insight. We end the session with a match-related drill.

In **session 2** we start with the same passing and shooting drill. However, the midfielders are now confronted by an opponent. In the training phase we take this drill with 2 lines further. The defensive midfielder (4) and one opponent join in. We end the session with a match-related drill.

Session 3: In the discovery phase, we take the passing and shooting drill further. More opposing players are included. In the training phase we expand the drill to 7v7 + goalkeeper. We end with a match-related drill against another team.

Session 4: We expand the passing and shooting drill to a drill with 2 lines (7v5 + goalkeeper). In the training phase we repeat the drill with 2 lines (7v7 + goalkeeper). We end with a match-related drill.

Session 5: In the discovery phase we work with the same drill again. The rest of the session is very match-specific: 11v11 against a younger team.

In matches, we see that the build-up functions smoothly again.

Session 1
Development objective of the session
In session 1 we start with a passing and shooting drill, with the focus on technical aspects (for switching the play from one flank to the other). In this drill, we work with specific positions from a real match. In the training phase we move to a drill with 2 lines (6v5 + goalkeeper). This combines technique and insight. We end the session with a match-related drill.

Discovery phase: Passing and shooting drill
Training phase: 6v5 + K
Game phase: Match-related drill (8v8, depending on the number of available players)

Content of the session
Discovery phase:
Passing and shooting drill

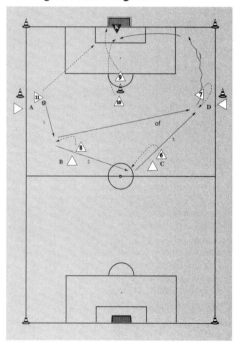

Organization:
Variation 1
- The winger (11) lays the ball back to the left midfielder (8).
- The left midfielder (8) plays the ball to the right midfielder (6).

- The right midfielder (8) plays the ball to the right winger (7).
- The winger (7) crosses the ball.
- We then start again on the other flank.

Variation 2
- The winger (11) lays the ball back to the left midfielder (8).
- The left midfielder (8) plays the ball directly to the right winger (7).
- The winger (7) crosses the ball.
- We then start again on the other flank.
- The striker, the withdrawn striker and the left winger take up positions in front of the goal.
- The players all stand in their specific positions.
- Vary the pass to the winger: pass to his feet; pass forward into space; pass along the ground; pass through the air.

Coaching points:
Winger (11)
- Play the ball in firmly (low and hard).
- Ensure that the midfielder can turn immediately.
- Communicate with the midfielder.

Left midfielder (8)
- Check away from the ball first.
- Do not stand too close to the winger.
- Turn as you receive the ball.
- Correct technique (firm – in front of the attacker – to feet – away from the defender).

Right midfielder (6)
- Do not stand level with the winger.
- Use the outside foot to receive the ball.

Winger (7)
- Take up position as far forward as possible (= space for the ball to be played into).
- Stand facing infield, with your back to the line.
- Leave space for the ball.
- Do not stand still.

Attackers in front of the goal
- Good role distribution.
- Near and far post.

Training phase: 6v5 + K

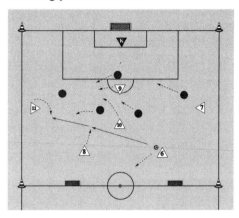

Organization:
- The attackers can score in the large goal.
- The defenders can score in one of the two small goals.

Defensive organization (see diagram)
The opposition's two defensive midfielders take turns to push forward toward the ball (this creates more space for the team in possession on the other flank = objective).

Coaching points:
- See passing and shooting drill.
- We try to switch the ball to the other flank as quickly as possible.
- If we can create dangerous situations in the penalty area, this is the first choice.
- The ball should not be switched from one flank to the other just for the sake of it.

Success moment:
- Successful switch from winger to winger = 1 pt.
- Goal in large goal = 2 pts.

Game phase:
8v8 (depending on the number of available players).
Free play.

Session 2
Development objective of the session
In session 2 we start with the same passing and shooting drill. However, the midfielders are now confronted by an opponent. In the training phase we take this drill with 2 lines further. The defensive midfielder (4) and one opponent join in. We end the session with a match-related drill.

Discovery phase: Passing and shooting drill
Training phase: 7v6 + K
Game phase: Match-related drill (11v11, depending on the number of available players)

Content of the session
Discovery phase:
Passing and shooting drill

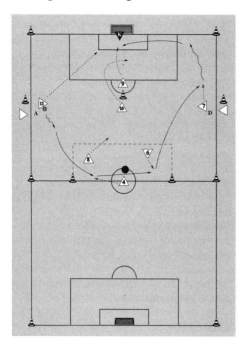

Organization:
The same organization as for the passing and shooting drill in session 1. The defender can win the ball and can score by dribbling it over an imaginary line. The midfielders try to switch the ball to the other flank. After the attempt to score, the sequence starts again from the other flank.

Coaching points:
Winger (11)
- Play the ball in firmly (low and hard).
- Ensure that the midfielder can turn immediately.
- Communicate with the midfielder.

Left midfielder (8)
- Check away from the ball first.
- Do not stand too close to the winger.
- Turn as you receive the ball.
- Correct technique (firm – in front of the attacker – to feet – away from the defender).

Right midfielder (6)
- Do not stand level with the winger.
- Use the outside foot to receive the ball.

Winger (7)
- Take up position as far forward as possible (= space for the ball to be played into).
- Stand facing infield, with your back to the line.
- Leave space for the ball.
- Do not stand still.

Attackers in front of the goal
- Good role distribution.
- Near and far post.

Training phase:
7v6 + K

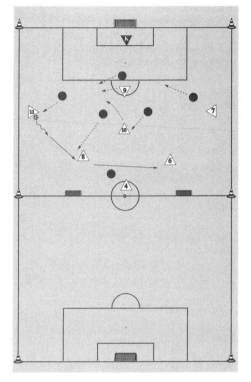

Organization:
- In this drill, the defensive midfielder (4) and another opponent are added.
- The attackers can score in the large goal.
- The defenders can score in one of the two small goals.

Defensive organization (see diagram):
The opposition's two defensive midfielders take turns to push forward toward the ball (this creates more space for the team in possession on the other flank = objective).

Coaching points:
- See passing and shooting drill.
- We try to switch the ball to the other flank as quickly as possible.
- If we can create dangerous situations in the penalty area, this is the first choice.
- The ball should not be switched from one flank to the other just for the sake of it.

Success moment
- Successful switch from winger to winger = 1 point.
- Goal in large goal = 2 points.

Game phase:
8v8 (depending on the number of available players).
Free play.

Session 3
Development objective of the session
Session 3: In the discovery phase, we take the passing and shooting drill further. More opposing players are included. In the training phase we expand the drill to 7v7 + goalkeeper. We end with a match related drill against another team.

Discovery phase: Passing and shooting drill
Training phase: 7v7 + K
Game phase: Match-related drill (11v11, depending on the number of available players)

Content of the session
Discovery phase:
Passing and shooting drill

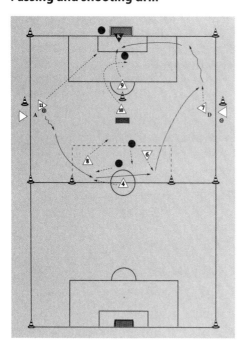

Organization:
Passing and shooting drill
- We expand the passing and shooting drill.
- The midfielders now have to deal with 2 opponents. Defender 1 stands in the zone, and defender 2 enters the zone if one of the midfielders wins the ball.
- The attackers try to switch the play from one flank to the other.
- After an attempt to score, we start again on the other flank.

Positions in front of the goal
- A defender tries to intercept the ball and score in the small goal.
- The three attackers try to score in the large goal.

Coaching points:
Winger (11)
- Play the ball in firmly (low and hard).
- Ensure that the midfielder can turn immediately.
- Communicate with the midfielder.

Left midfielder (8)
- Check away from the ball first.
- Do not stand too close to the winger.
- Turn as you receive the ball.
- Correct technique (firm – in front of the attacker – to feet – away from the defender).

Right midfielder (6)
- Do not stand level with the winger.
- Use the outside foot to receive the ball.

Winger (7)
- Take up position as far forward as possible (= space for the ball to be played into).
- Stand facing infield, with your back to the line.
- Leave space for the ball.
- Do not stand still.

Attackers in front of the goal
- Good role distribution.
- Near and far post.

Training phase:
7v7 + K

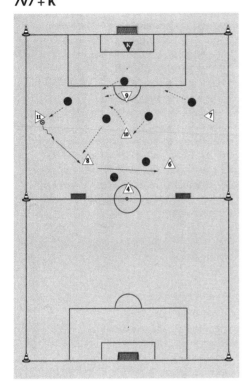

Organization:
- In this drill, another defender is added.
- The attackers can score in the large goal.
- The defenders can score in one of the two small goals.

Defensive organization (see diagram):
The opposition's two defensive midfielders take turns to push forward toward the ball (this creates more space for the team in possession on the other flank = objective).

Coaching points:
- See passing and shooting drill.
- We try to switch the ball to the other flank as quickly as possible.
- If we can create dangerous situations in the penalty area, this is the first choice.
- The ball should not be switched from one flank to the other just for the sake of it.

Success moment
- Successful switch from winger to winger = 1 point.
- Goal in large goal = 2 points.

Game phase:
11v11 (depending on the number of available players).
Free play.

Session 4
Development objective of the session
Session 4: We expand the passing and shooting drill to a drill with 2 lines (7v5 + goalkeeper). In the training phase we repeat the drill with 2 lines (7v7 + goalkeeper). We end with a match-related drill.

Discovery phase: Passing and shooting drill, then 7v5 + K
Training phase: 7v7 + K
Game phase: Match-related drill (8v8, depending on the number of available players)

Content of the session
Discovery phase:
Passing and shooting drill, then 7v5 + K

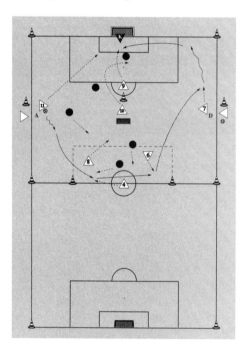

Organization:
Passing and shooting drill
- We expand the passing and shooting drill.
- The midfielders now have to deal with 2 opponents. Defender 1 stands in the zone, and defender 2 enters the zone if one of the midfielders wins the ball.
- One defender stays with the winger (11) when he plays the ball back.
- The attackers try to switch the play from one flank to the other.
- After the cross, the passing and shooting drill turns into 7v5 + goalkeeper.
- The defenders can score in the small goal.
- The attackers can score in the large goal.

Coaching points:
Winger (11)
- Play the ball in firmly (low and hard).
- Ensure that the midfielder can turn immediately.
- Communicate with the midfielder.

Left midfielder (8)
- Check away from the ball first.
- Do not stand too close to the winger.
- Turn as you receive the ball.
- Correct technique (firm – in front of the attacker – to feet – away from the defender).

Right midfielder (6)
- Do not stand level with the winger.
- Use the outside foot to receive the ball.

Winger (7)
- Take up position as far forward as possible (= space for the ball to be played into).
- Stand facing infield, with your back to the line.
- Leave space for the ball.
- Do not stand still.

Attackers in front of the goal
- Good role distribution.
- Near and far post.

Training phase:
7v7 + K

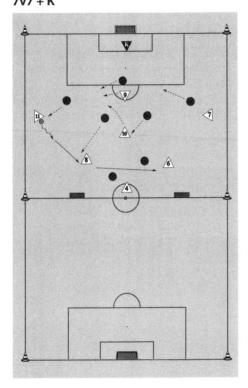

Organization:
- In this drill, another defender is added.
- The attackers can score in the large goal.
- The defenders can score in one of the two small goals.

Defensive organization (see diagram):
- The defenders always leave one midfielder free.
- The coach decides: 1 = 4 free, 2 = 6 free, 3 = 8 free.

Coaching points:
- See passing and shooting drill.
- We try to switch the ball to the other flank as quickly as possible.
- If we can create dangerous situations in the penalty area, this is the first choice.
- The ball should not be switched from one flank to the other just for the sake of it.

Success moment
- Successful switch from winger to winger = 1 point.
- Goal in large goal = 2 points.

Game phase:
8v8 (depending on the number of available players).
Free play.

Session 5

Development objective of the session

Session 5: In the discovery phase we work with the same drill again. The rest of the session is very match-specific: 11v11 against a younger team.

Discovery phase: 7v7 + K
Training and
Game phase: Match-related drill (11v11, depending on the number of available players)

Content of the session
Discovery phase:
7v7 + K

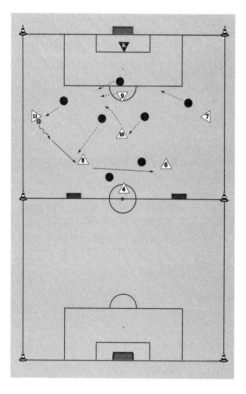

Organization:

- The attackers can score in the large goal.
- The defenders can score in one of the two small goals.

Defensive organization (see diagram):

- The defenders always leave one midfielder free.
- The coach decides: 1 = 4 free, 2 = 6 free, 3 = 8 free.

Coaching points:

- See passing and shooting drill.
- We try to switch the ball to the other flank as quickly as possible.
- If we can create dangerous situations in the penalty area, this is the first choice.
- The ball should not be switched from one flank to the other just for the sake of it.

Success moment

- Successful switch from winger to winger = 1 point.
- Goal in large goal = 2 points.

Training and game phase:
11v11

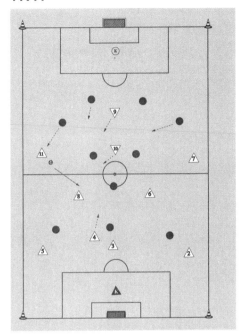

Organization:

Both teams play in a 1:4:3:3 formation. In the attacking team, a central defender (3 or 4) plays in front of the defense.

Task: Take advantage of the extra man and try to play the ball as quickly as possible to the wingers.

Evaluation

Problem-oriented coaching

Have the players enjoyed themselves?
There was sufficient variation in the drills.

Has there been an influence on the soccer problem?
Clear progress can be observed in matches. The players have clearly been influenced, as can be seen from the way the play is switched from one flank to the other.

Is the number of practice drills in the training sessions limited?
There are a maximum of 3 drills in each training session.

Is the number of practice drills in the module limited?
A total of 3 practice drills are integrated in the module.

Is there a good balance between match-related and non-match-related drills?
Only match-related drills are used. The choice of drills depends on the nature of the soccer problem.

Is there a progressive buildup over a certain period?
Five training sessions are completed over a period of 3 weeks. The level of difficulty of the drills is gradually increased.

Are there sufficient repetitions for the players?
All players are sufficiently involved in each drill.

Is sufficient consideration given to the age group of the players?
The drills used in these practical examples are oriented to the players' age group. The content is adjusted to the age of the players.

Are the drills adjusted to their level?
The drills are applicable at the highest youth level. If they are too difficult, the coach can easily adjust them.

Do the players have sufficient freedom of movement?
Sufficient free moments are incorporated.

Practice Drills

Passing and Shooting Drills

Passing and shooting drill

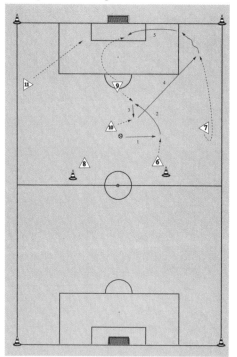

Development objective
Developing the technical skills (passing and shooting, receive and go, crossing) needed by the players in their own positions in relation to wing play.

Organization
- *All players in their own position.*
- *The withdrawn striker (10) plays the ball to the right midfielder (6).*
- *The right midfielder (6) plays the ball with his first touch to the striker (9).*
- *The striker (9) lays the ball off to the withdrawn striker (10).*
- *The withdrawn striker passes to the right winger (7).*
- *The right winger (7) crosses the ball.*
- *The striker (9) and the other winger (11) run in at the goal to meet the cross.*

Variations
- *Play the ball out to the other flank.*
- *The choice depends on the players.*

Success moment
10 balls. How often is a goal scored?

Coaching points
Right midfielder (6)
- *Look for space.*
- *Play the ball firmly to the striker.*
- *Play the ball away from the (imaginary) defender.*

Striker (9)
- *Check away to make space.*
- *Lay the off with the outside foot.*
- *Play the ball diagonally for the withdrawn striker to run onto.*

Withdrawn striker (10)
- *Do not move forward too soon.*
- *Look for space.*
- *Face the flank.*

Right winger (7)
- *Leave yourself space.*
- *Do not go forward too soon.*

Passing and shooting drill

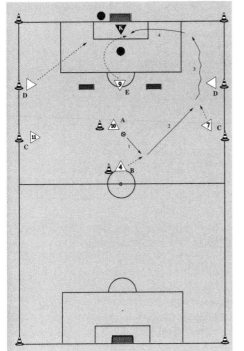

Development objective

Developing the technical skills (passing and shooting, receive and go, crossing) needed by the players in their own positions in relation to wing play.

Organization

- Player A lays the ball off to player B.
- Player B passes to winger C.
- Cross.
- Player E at the near post.
- Player D runs in at the far post.

- No defenders in front of the goal.
- 1 defender in front of the goal.
- 2 defenders in front of the goal.

Variations

- Play the ball forward directly.
- Make a run with the ball.
- Lay off and forward run.

Move up one place: A-B-C-D-E

Success moment

A headed goal counts double – who scores 5 goals first?

Coaching points

Player B
- Stand facing infield.
- Pass the ball so that the receiver can control it as easily as possible.
Player C
- Be aware of the overall situation.
- Position of the goalkeeper.
Player E
- Get in front of the goalkeeper.
- Do not run in too soon.
Player D
- Leave space for the cross.

Passing and shooting drill

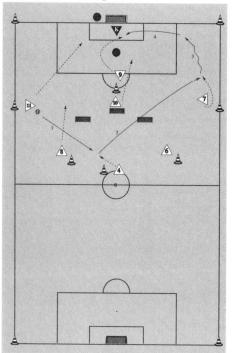

Development objective
Switching the play from one flank to the other and the possible variations in front of goal.

Organization
- *The left midfielder (8) makes a forward run.*
- *The left winger (11) plays the ball back to the defensive midfielder (4).*
- *The defensive midfielder plays the ball firmly (just over the goal) into the path of the winger (7), who is making a forward run.*
- *The winger (7) crosses the ball.*
- *The left winger (11), the striker (9) and the withdrawn striker (10) run in at the goal.*

Variations
- *Play the ball to the right midfielder (6), who plays it to the left midfielder (8).*

Running in at the goal:
- *Striker (9) runs toward the near or far post.*
- *The left winger (11) runs toward the near or far post.*
- *The withdrawn striker (10) takes up a position in the penalty area.*

Variations:
- *Play the ball forward directly.*
- *Make a run with the ball.*
- *Lay off and forward run.*
Move up one place: A-B-C-D-E

Success moment
A headed goal counts double – who scores 5 goals first?

Coaching points
Left winger (11)
- *Play the ball back firmly.*
Left midfielder (8)
- *Draw a defender.*
- *Take him with you when you run forward.*
Defensive midfielder (4)
- *Play the ball with the instep.*
- *Play the ball just over the goal.*
Winger (7)
- *Leave space in front of yourself.*

Passing and shooting drill

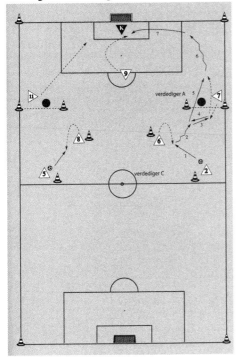

Development objective
Developing the technical skills (passing and shooting, receive and go, crossing) needed by the players in their own positions in relation to wing play.

Organization
- *We start alternately on the right and the left.*
- *The right midfielder (6) calls for the ball from the right back (2).*
- *The right midfielder (6) plays the ball to the right winger (7).*
- *The players then attempt to take the ball past the defender and cross the imaginary line by:*
    - *forward pass*
    - *playing the ball to the winger's feet*
    - *1-2 between the winger and the mid-fielder*
    - *overlapping run by the defender or the midfielder*

- *If the defender wins the ball, the sequence starts again.*
- *Cross (the striker (9) and the left winger (11) run in at the goal).*

Move up:
Follow the ball, or fixed positions.

Success moment
20 balls, alternately right and left; how often is a goal scored?

Coaching points
Defender (2 or 5)
- *Play the ball firmly.*
- *Communicate.*
Left midfielder (8)
- *Fake away from the ball.*
- *Receive and go.*
- *Play the ball forward directly or draw the defender (2v1 situation).*
Winger (7 or 11)
- *Be available for a forward pass or to receive a pass to your feet.*

Positional training

1v1
2v1
2v2
3v2
3v3
4v3
4v4
5v4
5v5   Game drill

1 v 1

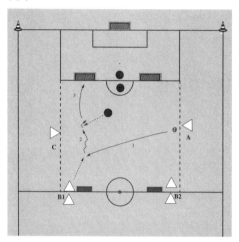

1 v 1 + K

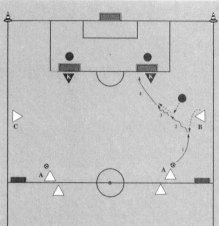

Development objective
Development of 1v1 play in attacking situations.

Organization
- Player A plays the ball to the incoming player B1.
- Player B1 tries to take the ball past the defender and score in one of the 2 small goals.
- Player C then starts by passing to the following player B2.
- Change positions. Passer and receiver change places, defender remains.

Success moment
If the defenders score 5 goals, other defenders are selected.

Coaching points
Winger
- Good first touch
- Attitude.
- Ensure you are up to speed when you receive the ball.
- Draw the defender in a given direction.

Development objective
Development of 1v1 play in attacking situations.

Organization
- We start alternately on the right and the left.
- Player A passes to the winger B.
- 1v1
- Winger B can score in the goal defended by a goalkeeper, and the defender can score in a small goal.

Success moment
Defenders against attackers. Who scores 5 goals first? If the defenders win, they can select the next defender.

Coaching points
Winger B
- Fake away from the ball first.
- Good first touch.
- Make a forward run with the ball.
- Threaten to go inside/outside.
- Time the fake or dribbling movement correctly.

2 v 1 + K

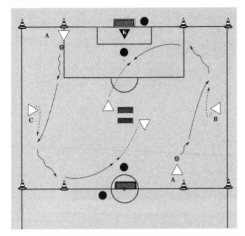

Development objective
Taking advantage of a 2v1 situation in front of the goal.

Organization
- *We work simultaneously on 2 flanks.*
- *Player A passes to the winger B.*
- *1v1 with the defender and cross the ball.*
- *The winger can score in the large goal.*
- *The defender can score in the small goal.*

Variations
- *Pass followed by a run with the ball.*
- *Pass, lay off, run onto forward pass.*
- *Pass and overlapping run.*

Success moment
Who scores 4 goals first?

Coaching points
Player A
- *Pass the ball firmly to the winger.*
- *Communicate with the winger.*

Winger B
- *Stand facing infield when you receive the ball.*
- *Look to see where the player in front of the goal is positioned.*

Player C (in front of the goal)
- *Be available.*
- *Get in front of the goalkeeper at the near post.*
- *Far post.*
- *Cut-back.*

131

2 v 2 + K

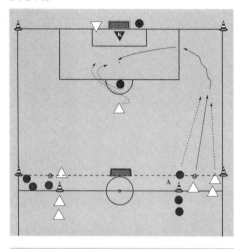

3 + K v 2 + K

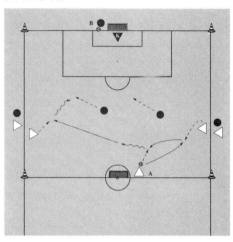

Development objective
Playing out a 2v2 situation on the flank/in front of the goal.

Organization
- We start on the right flank. A player from one team plays the ball forward. The defender starts with a slight disadvantage.
- We then play 2v2.
- The attackers can score in the large goal.
- The defenders can score in the small goal.
- We then start on the left flank.
- A player of the other team now plays the ball forward.
- The sequence is the repeated.

Success moment
Who scores 5 goals in the large goal first? Goals scored in the small goal are deducted from the total

Coaching points
- Try to cut across your opponent's path.
- Keep running.
- Stay in contact with the player in front of the goal.

Development objective
Playing out a 2v2 situation on the flank/in front of the goal.

Organization
- We start at goal A.
- Together with the two wingers, the player nearest the goal tries to get the ball past the two defenders (3v2 + goalkeeper).
- After a goal is scored, we restart at goal B. Now the other team has one player more.

Success moment
Which team scores 5 goals in the large goal first?

Variations
- Pass to the winger, who makes a run with the ball.
- 1-2 with support player.
- Support player makes overlapping run.

Players have to wait too long for their turn? Split the groups!

3 v 3 + K

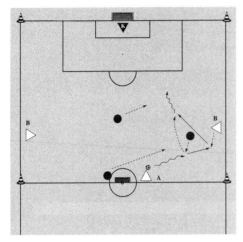

4 v 3 + K

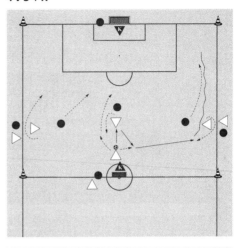

Development objective

Playing out a 3v3 + goalkeeper situation on the flank/in front of the goal.

Organization

- The third defender joins in when the support player plays the ball in.
- We then play 3v3 + goalkeeper.

Success moment

Goals scored with a first-time shot after dribbling past an opponent count double.

Coaching points

- Try to get the ball in front of the opposing team's goal as fast as quickly as possible (third defender).

Player A
- Play the ball in as quickly as possible.
- Pay attention to the pace of the ball.

Winger B
- Try to escape from your marker.
- Start your run with the ball as quickly as possible.
- Variations:
  - 1v1
  - 1-2 with support player.
  - Support player makes overlapping run.

Development objective

Playing out a 4v3 + goalkeeper situation on the flank/in front of the goal.

Organization

- We work with 2 x 2 teams.
- A team of four plus a goalkeeper plays against a team of 3 plus a goalkeeper.
- When a goal is scored, 2 new teams come into action.
- The team of four plus a goalkeeper then starts against the team of 3 plus a goalkeeper at the other goal.

Success moment

Goals scored with the first-time shot or header from a cross count double. Which is the first team to score 8 goals?

Variations

- 1v1
- 1-2 with striker.
- Support player makes overlapping run.

Be positive. Encourage the defender when he wins the ball rather than criticizing the attacker for losing it.

4 + K v 4 + K

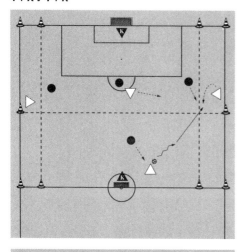

Game drill 5 v 5

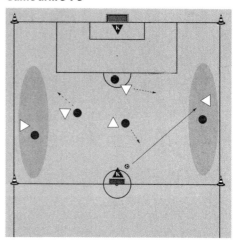

Development objective
Creating a scoring chance via the flank.

Organization
The field is divided into 2 halves. There is a zone 2 or 3 yards wide in the opposing team's half. The defender cannot enter this zone until the ball reaches the winger.

Success moment
Goals scored from a cross from the zone count double.

Coaching points
Player in possession
- *Pass the ball into space for the winger.*
- *Fast ball circulation – more time for the winger..*
- *Play the ball away from the defender.*

Winger
- *Keep moving, ready to run onto a pass.*
- *Be positive.*
- *Use the support player.*

Leave the drill to the players at first. Observe how they use the space and cope with difficulties.

Development objective
Creating a scoring chance via the flank.

Organization
Free play.

Task
- *Objective: To improve the winger's ability to dribble past an opponent on the outside.*
  - *The winger tries to dribble past the defender on the outside and cross the ball 3 times (the defenders are not told what the winger's task is).*
  - *How long does it take the winger to fulfill his task?*

Success moment
Goals scored from a cross count double. Who is the first to score 5 goals?

Give the players sufficient freedom of movement in the game drill.

Line training with 2 lines

6v4

6v5

6v6

7v6

7v7

8v7

8v8   Game drill

6 v 4 + K

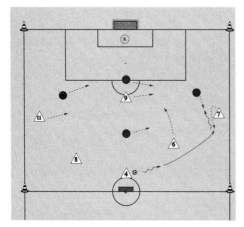

Development objective
Creating a scoring chance via the flank.

Organization
- *We play 6v4 + goalkeeper*
- *Before the winger starts a previously speci-fied movement, the defender must first touch the ground with both hands (= space for the winger to start a run with the ball).*

Success moment
The defenders lead 1-0. We play 6 minutes. If the attackers score twice, they win. We play 4 x 6 minutes. Who wins the game?

Coaching points
- *Make runs with the ball.*
- *Who is available in front of the goal?*

Working with completely free zones bears too little resemblance to a real game of soccer.

6 v 5 + K

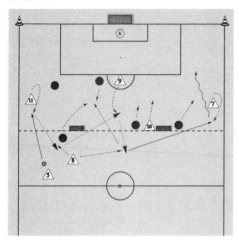

Starting by switching from one flank to the other encourages the players to try this in a match.

Development objective
Switching the play from one flank to the other; positions in front of the goal.

Organization
This drill is ideal for coaching positioning in front the goal. Depending on the strength of the attackers, the number of defenders can be increased or decreased. We start with a passing and shooting drill that then becomes a drill with opponents.
- *The left back (5) plays the ball to the left winger (11).*
- *The left winger (11) plays the ball back to the left midfielder (8), who passes to the striker (9).*
- *The striker (9) lays the ball off to the left midfielder (8).*
- *The left midfielder (8) passes to the right winger (7).*
- *The right winger (7) makes a run to the end line and crosses the ball.*

Positions in front of goal:
- *Striker (9) : Near post*
- *Withdrawn striker (10) : On and near the penalty spot.*
- *Left winger (11) : Far post.*
- *Left midfielder (8) : On and near the front edge of the penalty area.*

Each defender can join in after his immediate opponent has passed the ball. The attackers try to score in the large goal and the defenders can score in the two small goals. When a goal is scored, the players all go back to their starting positions. 5 and 8 swap places. After 8 sequences the drill is carried out on the other flank.

Success moment
Who scores 5 goals first?

Coaching points
See the positions in front of the goal.

6 + K v 6

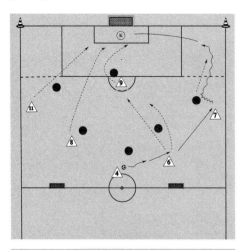

Development objective
Creating a scoring chance via the flank.

Organization
There is a zone about 15 meters deep. All
players can enter the zone when
- The attackers dribble the ball over the
  imaginary line.
- The attackers dribble the ball or receive a
  forward pass.
Attackers can score in the large goal.
Defenders can score in the two small goals.

Success moment
A goal scored directly after dribbling over the
imaginary line counts double.

Coaching points
- Try to create a 1v1 situation.
- Try to time the forward pass correctly.

The drill can be made easier or more difficult
by changing the formation of the defending
team.

7 + K v 6

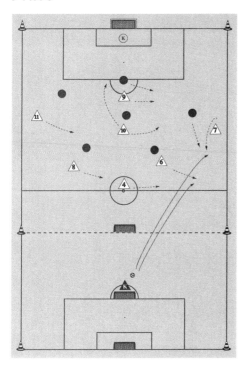

Development objective
Creating a scoring chance via the flank.

Organization
This drill focuses on the goalkeeper kicking the ball out to the winger, retaining posses-sion and the continuation. The goalkeeper has two choices:
- If a winger (7 or 11) is in space, he can send a long ball to him.
- He can also pass to one of the midfielders (6 or 8).

Attackers can score in the large goal. Defenders can score in the small handball goal.

Success moment
10 kick-outs – 2/3/4 goals?

Coaching points
- Take account of the ability of the wingers.
- Player is strong in the air = high ball.
- Player who can hold the ball = firm ball dropping into space in front of the player or aimed at his body.

The drill can incorporate goalkeeper coach-ing - the goalkeeper coach plays the ball to the goalkeeper, who sends a long ball forward.

7 + K v 7 + K

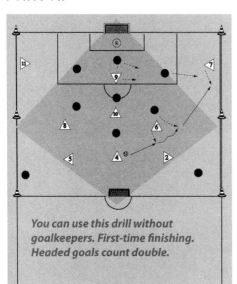

You can use this drill without goalkeepers. First-time finishing. Headed goals count double.

Game Drill 8 v 8

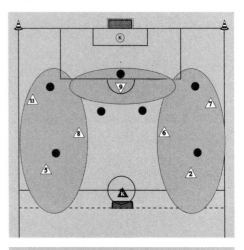

Development objective
Creating a scoring chance via the flank.

Organization
Each team has 2 wingers in the opposing team's half, where they can operate in the zone between the middle cone and the near post.

Success moment
Goal = 1 point, goal from a cross = 2 points.

Coaching points
- Try to reach the free player.
- Switch the play quickly from one flank to the other.

Development objective
Creating a scoring chance via the flank.

Organization
In own half = 2-touch play.
In opposing team's half = free play

Task
Objective: Improve forward passing into the space behind the defenders.
- Team A plays for offside.
- Team B tries to exploit the resulting space (through-pass).

Success moment
Headed goals count double.

Coaching points
Wingers
- Do not run forward too soon.
- Run wide first.

Player who passes the ball forward
- Try not to make the forward pass too predictable

Try to organize the game drill so that it is as close as possible to a real match.

Line training with 3 lines

9v6

9v7

9v8

9v9

10v8

10v9

10v10

11v10

11v11   Game drill

9 v 6 + K

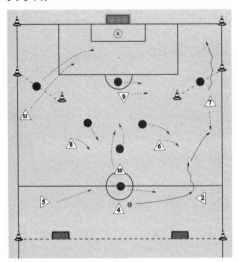

9 v 7 + 2K

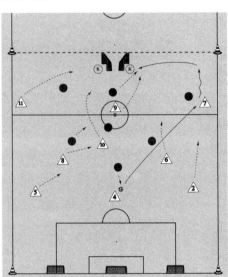

Development objective
Creating a scoring chance via the flank.

Organization
The 9-player team tries to score in the large goal. The 6-player team can score in the 2 small goals. Free play is permitted. The line defender can also defend the goal. When his immediate opponent has the ball, he defends the line.

Success moment
Goal = 1 point, goal after dribbling past the line defender = 2 points.

Coaching points
- Try to switch the play quickly from one flank to the other.
- Good positioning in front of the goal.

The winger's task can be made more difficult by positioning the defender in a zone. The winger must then dribble through the zone.

Development objective
To have fun.

Organization
The 9-player team can score in both goals. The 7-player team can score in the 2 handball goals (1 point). After 15 minutes the players switch roles. Who scores the most goals?

Success moment
Goal = 1 point; goal after a cross over the goal = 2 points.

Coaching points
- Try to get the ball to the winger as quickly as possible.
- Correct choice between long ball over the goal or shot at the first goal.

There may be some disagreement about whether this drill resembles real soccer situations, but there can be no doubting that the players enjoy it. Try it out.

9 v 8 + K

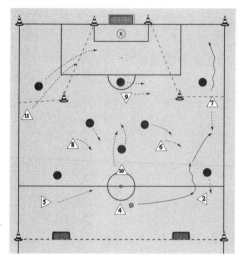

9 v 9 + K

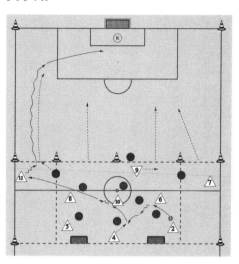

Development objective
Positions in front of the goal for a cross.

Organization
9 against 8 with a goalkeeper
- There are two zones at the sides of the field.
- The 9-player team can score points:
 - A goal from a cross is worth 2 points.
 - Any other goal is worth 1 point
- A defender can defend the zone.
- The defender need not remain in the zone.
- If the winger is supported in the zone by a teammate, his marker can also enter the zone.
- The 8-player team can score by dribbling the ball over the imaginary line.

Success moment
Goal = 1 point; goal from a cross = 2 points.
Who wins?

Coaching points
- Keep the space free for the winger.
- Try to switch the play quickly from one flank to the other.

Development objective
Creating a scoring chance via the flank.

Organization
- Play 7v7 in the central zone.
- The attackers try to take the ball past the defenders and play the ball to a winger in the right or the left zone.
- The winger's marker cannot challenge until the winger has received the ball.
- The winger tries to dribble past his marker. If he succeeds, the players all follow in the direction of the goal and we play 9v9.
- If the attackers score, we start again.
- The defenders can score in the small goals.

Success moment
The attackers have 2/3/4/5 minutes in which to score. How many goals do they score (minus the goals scored by the defenders)? The teams then swap roles. Which team has the most goals?

Coaching points
- Who is the free man?

10 v 8 + K

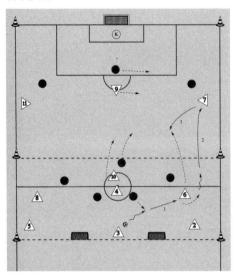

10 v 9 + K

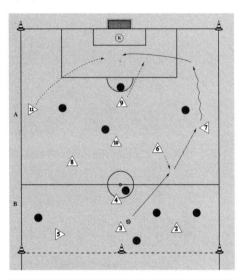

Development objective
Getting the ball to the free man and creating a scoring chance.

Organization
- There are 2 zones.
- 7v5 in zone A. If the 7-player team succeeds in getting the ball to a winger, 2 attackers and 1 defender can also enter the attacking zone B and we play 5v4 + goalkeeper.
- If the defenders win the ball in zone B, the zones no longer apply and we play 10 + goalkeeper v 8.
- The defenders can score in the 2 small goals.
- When a goal is scored, we start again.

Success moment
2-0 for the defenders, still 20 minutes to play.

Coaching points
- Patient build-up.
- Wait for the right moment to pass to the winger.

Development objective
Creating a scoring chance by switching the play from one flank to the other after winning possession.

Organization
- The defenders (the 9-player team) and the goalkeeper try to keep possession.
- Only 4 defenders and the goalkeeper are allowed in zone A.
- There are always 5 defenders in zone B.
- The attackers (the 10-player team) try to win possession and score in the large goal. There are no restrictions on their movement.

Success moment
If the defenders succeed in passing the ball 10/12/14 times, they are awarded one point. If the attackers score in the large goal, they are awarded one point.

Coaching points
- When possession is won, try to pass the ball forward as far as possible and as quickly as possible.
- Wingers stand facing infield.

10 + K v 10 + K

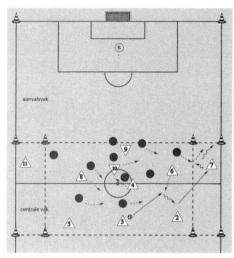

Game Drill 11 v 11

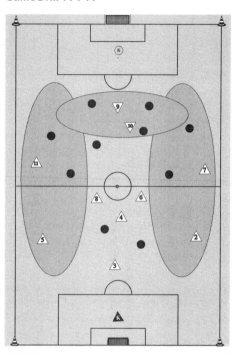

Development objective
Creating a scoring chance via the flank.

Organization
- We play 10v10 in the zone. There is a narrow strip along each side where the winger can only be challenged if he has the ball.
- If the winger succeeds in dribbling into the attacking zone, we play in both the attacking and the central zone.
- One attacking zone only ceases to exist when the opposing team succeeds in reaching the other one.
- A goal can be scored in the large goal.

Success moment
Who scores 5 goals first?

Variations
- Make a run with the ball.
- Play the ball forward for the winger.

Coaching points
- Try to get the ball to the winger as quickly as possible.
- Support the winger.

Development objective
Learning how to deal with a soccer problem.

Organization
Free play

Task
- Objective: The opposing team plays in a 1:4:4:2 formation. How do we deal with this?
  - Team A plays 1:3:4:3
  - Team B plays 1:4:4:2

Success moment
We play for 30 minutes. Who wins?

Coaching points
- Switch the play from one flank to the other as quickly as possible.
- The space is on the other flank.